Craft Beer

obsessions

Ian Coutts

Ian Coutts is the author of, amongst others, *The Perfect Keg* and *Brew North*, a lavishly illustrated history of beer and beer-drinking in Canada. He is a frequent contributor to *Taps: The Beer Magazine* and his writing has also appeared in *Toronto Life* and the *Globe and Mail*.

AUTHOR ACKNOWLEDGEMENTS: Thanks to Silvia Langford at Elwin Street, London. Thanks also to Tim Swingler in England, Erika Petersons in Australia and Chris Begley in Germany for their research assistance, and to Alan McLeod for reading the manuscript. Any remaining errors are mine. In Canada thanks to Ron Shore and Justin da Silva at Stone City Brewing, Andrew Connell at Bar Stillwell. In the United States, Jaime Jurado and Mark Wilson at Abita Brewing, Sam Calagione at Dogfish Head and Troy Parker at Bottle Caps Beverage Center in Watertown, NY. In the United Kingdom, Sam Smith at Samuel Smith's Brewery. Finally, thanks as always to my wife, Catharine Lyons-King.

Craft Beer

obsessions

Ian Coutts

hardie grant books

Contents

Why be obsessed with craft beer?

What do we talk about when we talk about craft beer? The definition can be stretched to include many candidates, from the obvious (the beers made by Sierra Nevada or BrewDog, for example), to those from centuries-old breweries that one might not immediately think of. In both cases, what we are talking about is well-crafted beer. But what makes craft beer 'craft'? It's partly in the ingredients – beer made from malt and hops, without corn syrup or rice to stretch it out.

It's also in the attitude – the ad campaign shouldn't take precedence over the fluid in the bottle. Craft beer is particular: it isn't a concocted beverage with some 'beer-like' attributes to please the largest possible audience. Craft makers are committed to beer, whether they are tattooed Portlandians with beards like Confederate generals or Trappist monks in a Belgian abbey. And, as it happens, those two images tap into craft beer's most interesting paradox: that great brewers are often traditional in outlook – when they aren't being insanely avant-garde.

Of course, craft beer makes you feel good, but all beer does that. And all beer, not just craft beer, makes others seem smarter and more attractive. These beers, however, have flavour. And aroma. And they combine them in complex and subtle ways. For those of us who came of age drinking industrial beers, it is

▲ A jewel-encrusted beer tap at the Dogfish Head Brewery, Milton, Delaware, USA.

▲ Pouring a Green Apple Wheat Beer by Quebec's Unibroue brewery.

a revelation: beer can taste like this? More than that, these obsession-worthy beers often come with a story – a long-forgotten style or a local connection, thanks to the ingredients or the location of the brewery.

Craft beers are also accessible. Sure, there are ones that can set you back as much as a good bottle of wine or more – Samuel Adams' Utopias, for instance, which comes out every two years, sells for $199 (US) per 700-ml (24-fl oz) bottle, but that is very much an exception. In general, unlike wine, cigars or Scotch, good beer isn't a lot more expensive than mediocre beer. And there aren't many areas in life in which that's true.

In a similar vein, beer is democratic. There are beer snobs out there, but thanks to its low cost and the fact that you can't really build up a vast cellar of dusty, ageing bottles (apart from a few unusual Belgian-style beers), it's hard to build up an aura around beer that chases away ordinary people. It probably helps that beer has proletarian or 'working-man' origins and craft beer hasn't lost that side of its personality. Beer is also a very social drink, and with craft beers and great traditional ones, if nothing else, you can discuss what's in your glass.

In addition, craft beer is open-ended. If you collect scrimshaw (yes, scrimshaw, you know, whale teeth engraved by nineteenth-century sailors), there are a finite number of pieces out there and, sooner or later, you'll have bought all you can afford or can get your hands on. They aren't making any more. Craft beer, on the other hand, is growing. Occasionally you'll hear rumblings from beer writers that we have hit 'peak' craft, but it hasn't happened yet.

There are new breweries and new beers along every day. In the UK and Europe, there are more breweries open today than at any time since the 1930s. In the United States, the Brewing Association estimates there are more open now than at any time since the 1870s. And these breweries are turning out everything from pale ales to sour beers and porters – you name it, you can find it. This is the golden age of beer. You probably couldn't drink one of every craft beer out there if you tried.

In that respect at least, the world of craft beer might seem a little daunting. Fortunately this little book will set you on your path, turning what might be a partial interest into a proper obsession.

1

Fundamentals

How to drink craft beer

▲ The highly polished brew tanks of the Sierra Nevada Brewery, Mills River, North Carolina, USA.

Brewers spend a lot of time making sure that the individual elements of their brews work together. They worry about its balance (how the malt and hops work together), or whether a certain yeast will work well with a certain malt. So when we like a beer and we want to figure out why we like it, we need to pick the beer apart to assess it.

The Beer Judging Certification Program in the United States has come up with a series of categories that help us break down the essence of a beer and then stick it all back together again in a straightforward fashion. Here's a simplified version: imagine a glass in front of you containing any sort of beer at all.

APPEARANCE How does it look in the glass? Can you describe the colour? How much head is there and how long does it last? Swirl it a little – do you get some residue of head on the side of the glass, an effect that is commonly known as 'lacing'? This is often associated with the degree of bitterness in a beer, which relates back to the quality of the hops used.

AROMA What can you smell? Mown grass? Citrus? Pine? A malty smell? Try to name the scents, and remember that a beer can have more than one aroma. You might be getting two at the same time – say, citrus and pine – or a dominant one combined with fainter traces, or 'notes', of others.

TASTE Human taste is a pretty simple sense. We basically have sweet, salty, bitter, acid and (arguably) umami, that mysterious fifth taste associated with glutamates and found in soy sauce, mushrooms and some fermented foods. But in a more colloquial sense, when we talk about taste we are including aroma. If you've ever done that trick where you hold your nose and then drink or eat something, you'll realize that you can't really taste things as effectively when you aren't getting the aroma, that we breathe in through our nose, but which also comes up the retronasal passage at the back of our throats. It is this miraculous passage that also enables us to blast beer through our nostrils when we laugh too hard.

▲ From left to right: a glass of London Stout, Yakima Red and London Pale Ale served in the tasting rooms at the Meantime Brewing Company in London, UK.

And – although they aren't really a part of taste – you might want to think about mouthfeel and carbonation, as they both affect the way we perceive a beer.

So what are you getting? What's the biggest flavour? Bitter, obviously, but that is true of almost all beers. What else? Do any flavours carry over from the aroma? Is there any residual sweetness? Is there a yeasty, bready flavour? Something like pine? See if you can get the right words for it.

In the 1970s, American and European brewers got together to create what they called a flavour wheel, which tries to give beer a shared vocabulary of taste and scent. It defines 17 tastes and 24 aromas and breaks these categories down further – acid, in the taste category, for example, is broken down into sour, acetic and acidic. You don't really need to know these categories to assess beer, although they might come in handy when you are reading other people's tasting notes on beer.

That first sip tells you a lot, but what else are you getting? Is there a finish, or an aftertaste? This is a complex business and there is more going on in a beer than you realize – even in the case of beers you have been drinking and enjoying for years. For truly great tasters, each sip is part of a bigger story with a beginning, middle and end.

Finally, what is your overall impression? How does it all work together – or how does it fail to? Can you sum up the experience? Can you draw an analogy between this beer and other beers?

▲ Greg Engert, Beer Director at ChurchKey restaurant in Washington, DC, USA, presides over a tasting event.

How we drink the beer is a key part of the flavour experience as well. Beer should be cold – but never freezing. Generally, the more complex the beer, the warmer it should be drunk: lagers and pale ales taste best at 5–8°C, farmhouse ales and abbey styles at 7–9°C and British cask-conditioned bitters at 11–13°C (the so-called cellar temperature).

Most of us keep beer in the fridge, so drinking it at the right temperature means taking it out and giving it enough time to warm up slightly. A lager can be drunk straight from the fridge, but you might have

Beer in brief

You don't need an enormous vocabulary to enjoy beer, but there are a few terms that are key to know before we get started.

MALT Grain that has been soaked to start it germinating. Doing so releases the enzyme that will convert its starches to sugars. After it has been soaked, the malt is then dried at low heat to halt this process. When added to hot water (in what is known as the mash tun), the enzyme starts the conversion.

YEAST Yeast consumes the sugar from the malt and converts it to alcohol, producing carbon dioxide in the process. Yeasts also create esters during fermentation that add distinctive flavours. There are two dominant types: *Saccharomyces cerevisiae*, a top-fermenting yeast responsible for ales, and *Saccharomyces pastorianus*, a bottom-fermenting yeast responsible for lagers. There are numerous strains of both these yeasts, each producing a slightly different beer. In addition to these yeasts, there are wild yeasts, notably *Brettanomyces.*

HOPS The cones of the female hop plant were originally added to beer as a preservative. Hops are responsible for beer's trademark

bitterness and also provide beers with distinctive aromas and flavours, including pine and citrus.

WATER Called 'liquor' when used in the brewing process. Water can affect flavour in interesting ways. Most notably, hard water tends to bring out hoppy flavours, as in pale ales. Lagers, on the other hand, generally work best when made with soft water.

WORT Pronounced 'wirt', this term describes the result when the hot liquor is combined with the malt, in what is known as 'mashing in'.

THE BOIL The process of bringing the wort to the boil and adding the hops after all the starches have been converted to sugars.

PITCHING The process of adding the yeast. After the wort is cooled and the temperature is right, yeast is added (or pitched). At this point, the yeast gets to work making the beer.

▼ Pale malt for brewing beer. Barley isn't the only grain that can be malted – malted wheat is used in a number of beers – but only malted barley is referred to as 'malt'.

to wait an hour before you open a barley wine. With some beers it is probably easier not to put them in the fridge at all – a cold room or the cellar of your house would keep them at the ideal temperature.

What we drink beer out of is important too (see the glassware section on page 20). The glass should first be rinsed with cold water to get rid of any dust or vestigial soap, and also to prevent the beer from foaming too much.

Most of us think we don't really need a lesson in how to pour beer into a glass, but there are ways to do it that ensure a nice head and prevents the beer from overflowing the glass. Tilt the glass at a 45-degree angle and start pouring the beer in, close to the brim. (I was always taught to pour aiming for my thumb – but this assumes you aren't using a stemmed glass.) Once the glass is about halfway full, straighten it up and continue the pour. This should create a nice head on the beer.

Nonic   Tulip   Shaker   Mug

Glassware

If you are the sort of beer drinker who, when offered a glass for beer, quips that it already has one, then the question of which glass to drink from might seem irrelevant. This isn't so; the glass you use plays a part in your experience of the beer you are drinking. Some of this is purely aesthetic – but in other ways, the choice of glass affects the taste. Glassware has evolved differently to suit different beer styles. There are plenty of glasses out there – from huge German steins that can hold a litre, to the stemmed tulips used in Belgium and the narrow 200-ml glasses used for Kölsch – but there are, generally, three main styles.

First, there's the pint glass, generally taken to mean an English pint of 20 fl oz (as opposed to its American cousin of 16 fl oz. The nonic (pronounced 'no-nick'), the most common pint glass, features a slight bulge about two-thirds of the way up, which makes it easier to stack and gives it additional strength.

Other glasses include the tulip, a gently flaring version of the pint glass, and the shaker pint, which tapers up from the base (and was designed to act as one half of a Boston cocktail shaker).

In England, a very long time ago, the standard pint glass was a thick-walled, dimpled pint mug with a handle. Popular with publicans because the dimpling meant they were easier to hold on to when washing and the thick glass meant fewer got broken, these glasses slowly began fading away as automatic dishwashers became more common. Recently they appear to have gained a certain hipster credibility, and seem to be making a comeback.

Pilsner   Weissbier   Snifter   Chalice

Pint glasses are all good for bitters, pale ales, stouts, porters and other beers with generally lower alcohol contents – up to the strength of a double pale ale (about 9 per cent alcohol by volume). You can get your nose in there, a key part of their flavour, and get a lot of beer washing across your tongue.

Then there is a range of narrow glasses, in three types: the pilsner, the narrow pint and the *weissbier* glass. These glasses are designed to show off the lighter colour of the beer in them, and also to hold in their carbonation (a key part of their characters), particularly in the case of pilsner. The narrow *weissbier* helps distribute the particles in the beer that give it its characteristic 'cloudy' look.

Finally, there are stemmed glasses: the snifter, the chalice and a smaller version of the tulip. They hold less than both pints and narrow glasses and are suited to beers with fairly high alcohol contents – abbey and Trappist ales and barley wines. The smaller glass lets you warm the beer with your hand and swirl it to release the beer's aromas. The wide lip lets you savour the beer's strong flavours.

Getting serious about craft beer doesn't require a ruinous investment in glassware. (Although, that said, the German company Spiegelau turns out a nice set of four craft beer glasses that are a trifle pricey – although they are so delicate as to seem almost invisible; it's like having the beer sitting in the air in front of you.) Generally, you can get by with some pint glasses, a second set of narrow glasses for weisses and pilsners, and a single set of stemmed glasses – wine glasses would work just fine.

Always rinse the glasses with cold water before pouring.

Home brewing & beyond

If you are interested in craft beer, at some point you might want to consider brewing your own, although not as a way of cutting costs – if you get far enough in to home brewing, you can spend more than you ever imagined. How much? It's a safe bet that your children will never attend university.

At its heart, beer is pretty simple; essentially water, hops, malt and yeast. Sort of like the blues, another deceptively simple thing. The blues is just twelve bars and, generally, three chords, but it is capable of almost endless variations. Beer is the same: change the hops and you can make the beer more bitter or more floral; use different malts and you will alter the colour and the sweetness. You can take a recipe but use a different yeast, add fruit or cane sugar, or substitute malt with malted wheat, and it changes the result incredibly.

It isn't hard to get started as a home brewer – you just need a large container, one that can hold upwards of 20 litres (5 American gallons), and a starter kit. These kits are good for a start, but as you get better, you can try brewing with a mixture of malt extract and ground malts, moving on to creating beers using all-grain recipes. Maybe you'll start growing your own hops or brewing using wild yeasts. Honestly, all it takes is a systematic approach and a decent degree of cleanliness, and you should be able to turn out excellent brews.

The more you brew, the more you'll be able to unpack other people's beers and figure out the malts they used, what hops and how many other ingredients may have been added. You'll also likely develop a real respect for what they have accomplished.

Attend any major home-brewing event, the kind where the brewers get together to show off their chops, and you'll notice that the judges are often professional brewers from good craft breweries. Partly it's a courtesy – they're helping the people who are also their biggest fans – but partly they are there to learn: home brewers are the R&D division of the craft-brewing industry. Those dedicated amateurs, out there in their kitchens or garages, are brewing today what the rest of us will be drinking a few years from now. They push the limits and take the chances – and if something doesn't work out, well, it's only a few litres of beer. Plenty of people in the craft beer world got their start as home brewers, and then scaled up. Get good enough, and who knows? Maybe you could become a master craft brewer too.

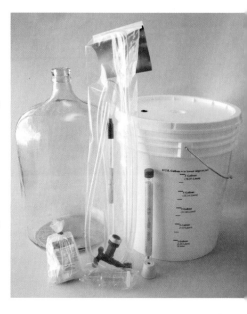

▲ Starter kits for home brewing are available and usually easy to use.

2

Pale Ales

The story of pale ale

▶ Despite the name, pale ales aren't all that pale. They range from golden brown to deep cherry. When they first appeared, however, they seemed pale in comparison to other beers.

'And I looked, and behold a pale ale.'

All right, that's not *exactly* what it says in Revelation. But these days anyone looking about them in a bar or pub, one that serves good beer, would certainly behold a lot of pale ale. Many very different beers, but all carrying the name pale ale. Of course, one of the things about beer is that the names aren't like appellations in French wine. You can call anything a pale ale, or an India Pale Ale (IPA), if you want to.

Even within the realm of craft beer, however, the term pale ale covers a whole spectrum of beers: American pale ales, English pale ales (called plain pale ales or bitters in England), Belgian pale ales, and then a whole range of India Pale Ales – referred to variously as American IPAs (further categorized as West-Coast and East-Coast IPAs), English IPAs, even double or imperial IPAs. Pale ales range from 3.5 per cent alcohol by volume right up to 10 per cent. These days, any craft brewer with any sort of pretensions will turn out a pale ale.

Pale ales can be traced back to the 1600s, but they really started to take off in the late eighteenth and early nineteenth centuries, thanks to a happy string of events. It's easy to vanish down the rabbit hole when talking about the history of pale ales, so what follows is just a brief history.

By the turn of the nineteenth century there was a strong potential market for beer among the soldiers and clerks busily creating the British Empire in India. But the beer needed to arrive there drinkable after a long sea voyage. So brewers created an ale that was high in alcohol (which meant it fermented slowly during the voyage out) and very heavily hopped to stop it from going bad. The beer was made using malt that had been roasted by indirect kilning, which gave more usable grain to brew with and left it paler in colour.

As it so happened, brewers in Burton-on-Trent made beer using hard water pumped from underground, and which was rich in gypsum and other salts. The ensuing beer had a clear, light taste, and the hard water brought out the hops' full flavour. It didn't hurt that the new beer looked good in the glassware that was becoming popular in the nineteenth century.

One producer, Bass, began exporting this India Pale Ale around the world. The new beer made inroads into North America, particularly Canada, and dominated England, where pub customers would order the beer by requesting 'bitter'.

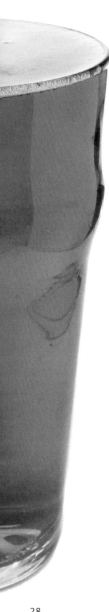

Pale ale versus bitter

Bitter remained the dominant beer in England and Wales throughout the nineteenth century and into the twentieth, but it started undergoing changes that shifted it away from traditional pale ales, in particular during the outbreak of the First World War when the British government reduced the permissible amount of alcohol in beer. Henceforth, regular bitter would be 3.5 per cent alcohol by volume. What came to be called 'special bitter' weighed in at about 4.0–4.5 per cent, and what brewers ultimately called their 'extra-special bitter' hit 5.5 per cent.

By the 1960s, in its pure manifestation, bitter was also endangered – thanks to big breweries that didn't want to bother with finicky cask-conditioned beverages that went bad quickly (see Cask versus Keg on page 100) when they could be selling highly carbonated, albeit bland, ales that lasted forever instead. Fewer pubs stocked it and fewer of the old independent breweries survived.

That you are reading a book about being obsessed with craft beer today is in part the result of one organization's efforts. Founded in 1971, the Campaign for Real Ale – or CAMRA, as it is more generally known – holds festivals, publishes a good beer guide and helped save cask ale. CAMRA has become the butt of jokes in recent years, but its role in the craft-beer revolution was a pivotal one. Saving good beers is as important as creating them.

Pale ale reborn

Pale ale's central place in the craft-beer pantheon can be traced to the American West Coast in the late 1970s and the births of the first American craft breweries. There wasn't an American tradition that these early brewers wanted to draw on, so they looked abroad for their inspiration. Most of these neophyte beer makers were also trying to create beers relatively inexpensively, and creating lager requires fairly expensive refrigeration, so pale ale was a good choice. But they weren't content simply mimicking older styles or reproducing them exactly; they wanted to play with them.

In November 1981, the Sierra Nevada Brewing Company introduced its Pale Ale, made with cascade hops from the American northwest. The citrusy aroma they gave the beer, along with a bitter finish, set the standard for subsequent American pale ales, with brewers all over the United States competing with each other to increase the alcohol content and make ever more heavily hopped beers – often to the point of undrinkability. Brewers in other parts of the world followed the American lead, even in the United Kingdom, closing the pale ale circle.

Can't Fight the Funk   ABV: 6.2%
BREWCULT, MELBOURNE, VICTORIA

This one is like the premise of a wacky beer sitcom – what happens when a hoppy IPA and a cellary saison find themselves in the same bottle? Well, it starts sweet but ends with a nice dry finish – all kicked off by floral notes. And bitter? Ha, you'd be bitter too! Hopped like an IPA, but with a saison yeast and grain bill, it really is a farmhouse IPA.

Hop Hog   ABV: 5.8%
FERAL BREWING, BASKERVILLE, WESTERN AUSTRALIA

Consistently voted Australia's best craft beer; in fact, about the only award Hop Hog hasn't won is the Nobel Prize. This is an American-style IPA with strong pine needle and citrus aromas, followed by an aggressive bitterness and dry finish. Aussie sources praise its bitterness, but add, 'it's not in-your-face bitterness that makes you pucker up or gives you that sandpaper-on-your-tongue feel'.

Original Pale Ale   ABV: 4.5%
COOPERS BREWERY, ADELAIDE, SOUTH AUSTRALIA

You can't write anything about Aussie beers without mentioning Coopers. Situated between craft and mainstream, they're the original when it comes to doing something differently. Their aptly named Original Pale Ale is cloudy (Coopers goes for fermentation in the bottle) and floral. There is generally a hoppiness to the beer, but nothing too heavy. A great all-rounder.

Pacific Ale   ABV: 4.4%

STONE & WOOD, BYRON BAY, NEW SOUTH WALES

This is another Australian take, an American-style
ale, one that, thanks to a relatively low alcohol
content, makes for a good session beer. Pacific Ale
is characterized by lovely fruity flavours: crisp with
hints of pineapple in a hazy, sunny-yellow beer.
A great ale to have on a hot day, it is also a perfect
gateway beer to introduce friends who are still
drinking the mainstream brewers to the pleasures of
craft beer.

Bone Shaker   ABV: 7.1%

CANADA

AMSTERDAM BREWING COMPANY, TORONTO, ONTARIO

Amsterdam is a relatively conservative
brewer, so this beer marks a real departure.
Bone Shaker is a dark reddish-brown, unfiltered
IPA that pours surprisingly clear. There's a
hint of fruit in the aroma, together with a hint
of feet (no joke) and even cardboard – but it
works. The dominant flavours are grapefruit
and hops – with a satisfyingly sour grapefruit-
rind finish.

CANADA ## Fat Tug ABV: 7%

DRIFTWOOD BREWERY, VICTORIA, VANCOUVER ISLAND

Arguably the best IPA made in Canada. Grapefruit, mango, melon – all are common in these Northwest/West Coast/Pacific IPAs, and Fat Tug is no exception. Brewed in Victoria on Vancouver Island this IPA weighs in with a mighty 80 IBUs (International Bittering Units); if the Americans had succeeded in getting the border pushed north back in the 1840s, this might be Washington state's top beer today.

Mad Tom ABV: 6.4%

MUSKOKA BREWING COMPANY, BRACEBRIDGE, ONTARIO

This is a reddish-gold IPA with a good head but not much lacing. There is a charming hint of bubblegum in the aroma. The bubblegum is in the flavour too, but it's under the hops, and the beer finishes off with a great taste of sour grapefruit.

Tankhouse Ale ABV: 5.2%

MILL STREET BREWING COMPANY, TORONTO, ONTARIO

Mill Street brew master Joel Manning calls this a 'Canadian' pale ale, presumably to differentiate it from its hoppier and lighter-coloured American cousins. A deep copper-red in colour, Tankhouse uses five malts in the brewing process combined with Cascade hops, which gives a bitterness to what is otherwise quite a malty beer.

Dead Pony Club India Pale Ale

ABV: 3.8%

BREWDOG BREWING, ELLON, ABERDEENSHIRE, SCOTLAND

Created by the guys who put the 'extreme' in extreme brewing, this is a thoroughly British take on the American West Coast pale ale. Brewed with three type of hops (including Citra and Simcoe, mainstays of American pale ales), Dead Pony Club boasts a surprisingly modest alcohol content, which makes it a good session ale. Of course, Brewdog being Brewdog, they also brew an extreme IPA, Hardcore, which boasts an ABV of 9.2 per cent and a tastebud-frying 125 IBUs (International Bittering Units).

Fuller's Extra Special Bitter

ABV: 5.9%

FULLER SMITH & TURNER, LONDON, ENGLAND

Anyone interested in an excellent example of a British bitter (either in bottle or cask) could do worse than Fuller's Extra Special Bitter. A favourite of CAMRA, who have named it Britain's best beer three times, Fuller's ESB boasts a sweet caramel, malty flavour with a hint of hop bitterness. Fullers invented the term 'extra-special bitter' for this beer when they started brewing it back in the early 1970s; today it is a recognized beer style, brewed worldwide.

UNITED KINGDOM

Heady Topper ABV: 8%
THE ALCHEMIST, WATERBURY, VERMONT

There are two schools of thought when it comes to Heady Topper: some people say it's the best beer in the world; others claim it's the best beer in the universe. There is no middle ground. This is an amazingly fruity IPA made with six different kinds of hops that, while obviously hoppy, isn't overpowering in the way that double IPAs often can be. Good luck finding it, though.

Pliny the Elder ABV: 8%
RUSSIAN RIVER BREWING, SANTA ROSA, CALIFORNIA

Often regarded as the greatest American double IPA, its relative scarcity probably plays a part in boosting the mystique around Pliny the Elder. Most fans will tell you to believe the hype – it's got the piny, citrusy, West-Coast thing happening, but it's also surprisingly well balanced – despite boasting an awe-inspiring 100 IBUs (International Bittering Units). Best drunk fresh – but hard to find. Russian River also produces a Pliny the Younger with an ABV of 11 per cent.

Sierra Nevada Pale Ale

ABV: 5.6%

SIERRA NEVADA BREWING COMPANY, CHICO, CALIFORNIA

This is arguably the 'ale zero' of the craft-beer revolution. Pale ales have gone in many directions since company founder Ken Grossman started brewing back in early the 1980s, but Sierra Nevada's citrusy aroma and nice hop bite still hold up today.

60 Minute India Pale Ale   ABV: 6%

DOGFISH HEAD BREWERY, MILTON, DELAWARE

This India Pale Ale was created using what the firm founder Sam Calagione refers to as their 'continuous hopping' method – 60 additions of citrusy and piny American hops over the course of an hour-long boil. The result is a beer with great citrus and floral notes and a solid malty taste that is well balanced, and definitely not overwhelmed by the hops. Dogfish Head also produces 75- and 120-minute IPAs.

Stone India Pale Ale   ABV: 6.9%

STONE BREWING COMPANY, ESCONDIDO, CALIFORNIA

The San Diego region of southern California is home to many imaginative craft brewers, of which the largest and best known is Stone Brewing Company. Their IPA is often held up as the epitome of what a West Coast IPA should be – spicy, piny and citrusy aromas combined with a bitter but, paradoxically, clean finish.

3

Amber, Brown & Other Ales

Amber, brown & cream ales

Pale ales seem to command most of the attention these days, but they are not the whole story. Even if you follow tradition, and exclude stouts and porters from a discussion of ales, there are still a vast number of ales out there.

Historically, in England, 'ales' were beers brewed without hops. 'Beers' used hops, a dangerous foreign import. Over time, however, English brewers began using hops in their ale so that distinction was lost. The easiest definition today is that beers are brewed with a top-fermenting yeast, generally some strain of *Saccharomyces cerevisiae* (which is also used in winemaking and baking).

It should be noted, for the pedants among us, that this is something of an over-simplification.

Amber & red ales

The Beer Judge Certificate Program spends a lot of time trying to make the various categories of beer work. According to its standards, an American Amber should be 25–40 IBU (International Bittering Units) and 4.5–6.2 per cent ABV. Oh, and amber, of course. This is fine, until you discover that a lot of the beers that call themselves red or amber – Tröegs Nugget Nectar and Bear Republic Red Rocket Ale,

▶ Taking a sample from the keg, Hofbräuhaus, Traunstein, Germany.

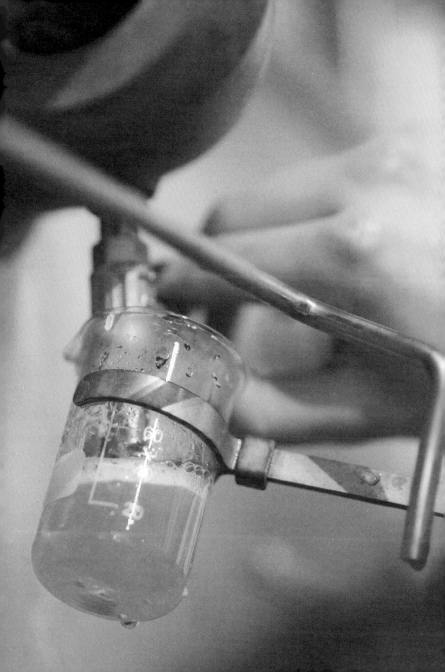

to name two excellent beers – aren't red ales by this standard, even though they claim to be. They are just too hoppy and too high in alcohol. It's almost as if these red ales are born with a secret desire to be IPAs. This is just one of those places where the categories have bent and stretched in odd ways. That aside, there are some good American reds or ambers out there that fit the BJCP description.

Brown ales

Once upon a time, pretty much every ale was a brown ale. Before refinements in kilning technology, there was no way to avoid roasting malt until it was quite dark. Generally, a brown ale in the UK was about 5 per cent alcohol by volume and often characterized by caramel, toffee or nut flavours. Newcastle Brown Ale is probably the most common, commercialized version of this venerable beer. Oddly enough, today the place where you're likeliest to find these classic brown ales is the United States, where a whole range of brewers make them.

Cream ales

Cream ales are often slotted in to the hellish category known as 'lawnmower beers' – meaning you can drink one while doing gardening on a Saturday afternoon without too much danger of removing a foot. Originally created to compete with then newly popular lagers in North America, and historically fermented at much lower temperatures than most ales, they are low in alcohol, low in hoppiness and generally low in maltiness, too. Bland? Please, we prefer subtle.

Cameron's Cream Ale ABV: 5%   CANADA
CAMERON'S BREWING COMPANY, OAKVILLE, ONTARIO

The Cream Ale was the first beer ever produced by the company and has earned a few awards over the years (including a gold in the Cream Ale category at the Canadian Brewing Awards in 2009, beer of the year and gold at the 2009, 2012 and 2013 United States Open Beer Championships). This light-coloured beer has a malty, sweet aroma and a malty, almost bready flavour with a grassy finish.

UNITED KINGDOM

Samuel Smith's Nut Brown Ale

ABV: 5%

**SAMUEL SMITH BREWERY, TADCASTER,
NORTH YORKSHIRE, ENGLAND**

One of those baseline beers that all others are measured against. Fermented in what are known as 'stone Yorkshire squares' (box-like fermenting vessels made of slate), this Nut Brown Ale features flavours of raisin, nut, caramel and some fruit. Not only that, it's certified vegan too.

UNITED STATES

Carnie Fire   ABV: 5%

**COAST BREWING COMPANY, NORTH CHARLESTON,
SOUTH CAROLINA**

This brew, available each autumn as a seasonal ale, pushes all the buttons as a genuine American amber. A slightly cloudy amber with ruby accents and a tremendously long-lasting head, Carnie Fire has peach, caramel and piny (almost resiny) aroma notes. Its flavour is best described as malty and caramel, with a grapefruit-rind aftertaste.

El Toro   ABV: 4%

FULLSTEAM BREWERY, DURHAM, NORTH CAROLINA

A fascinating beer from a fascinating brewery with true dedication to their region and local produce. In this case, that means good old Southern corn grits, which combine with two-row barley to create the grain bill for this cream ale.

Nut Brown Ale ABV: 5%

ALESMITH BREWING COMPANY, SAN DIEGO, CALIFORNIA

San Diego's AleSmith proves that a brown ale needn't be made in England to be English. Their Nut Brown Ale features a nutty aroma and a malty, almost bready flavour to which the hops add a grassy finish. Not too widely available and produced on a rotating basis, this is one you'll definitely have to hunt down.

Palo Santo Marron ABV: 12%

DOGFISH HEAD BREWERY, MILTON, DELAWARE

Dark brown, verging almost on black, *palo santo* means 'holy tree' in Spanish. In this case it refers to a type of wood grown in Paraguay, commonly used in making wine casks (here, the vessels the beer is fermented in). This unfiltered brown ale is characterized by aromas of caramel and vanilla and flavours of molasses and brown sugar.

Rogue Hazelnut Brown Nectar
ABV: 6.2%

ROGUE ALES, NEWPORT, OREGON

Eight malts, combined with two types of hops and hazelnut, give this brown ale from Rogue Ales a rich, nutty flavour (including, not at all surprisingly, hazelnut), combined with a malty finish. Fans also report aromas of chocolate and roasted malt.

Sweet Action   ABV: 5.2%

SIXPOINT BREWERY, BROOKLYN, NEW YORK

Sixpoint's website points out that 'Beer is culture', by which this brewery means that its invention has been responsible for – well, everything good ever. This cream ale lives up to its name, with a lot of floral hoppiness in the aroma that combines with an almost peachy flavour – sweet up front, followed by a hoppy finish.

Tröegs Hopback Amber Ale

ABV: 6%

TRÖEGS BREWING COMPANY, HERSHEY, PENNSYLVANIA

It's relatively small city, but Hershey and its environs are home to something like a dozen craft breweries. A hopback is a container filled with whole leaf hops that the wort is pumped through while brewing to guarantee a really strong hop content. This amber ale features no fewer than four kinds of hops, with Nugget and Crystal in the hopback.

◀ Inside a tank at the Sixpoint Brewery in Brooklyn, New York, USA.

Creating a new beer

Every day a craft brewer seems to dream up a new beer or a new take on an existing brew – rye IPAs, vanilla stouts, imperial you-name-it, the proliferation never seems to end. And if mainstream brewers are content to turn out the same beer year after year, then a trademark of craft brewing is that it is forever changing.

Justin da Silva is the brew master at Kingston, Ontario's Stone City Ales. Opened in 2014, this prize-winning craft brewery has gained a growing reputation for its special releases, more than 30 in their first year of operation alone, ranging from saisons to Belgian IPAs to Berlin weissbiers to an unforgettable Christmas beer featuring cranberries (and actual spruce branches), almost all the product of da Silva's imagination.

'Usually,' he says in explaining how he picks what to brew, 'it's a style that I want to drink, or that the brewing staff want to drink. I try to take the concept and make it my own, craft it how I picture it might taste.'

With more common beers, creating a new recipe is fairly straightforward. For example, 'with double IPAs,' says da Silva, 'those beers are all about hops. So you don't want to load up too much on the grain bill to take away from that. You go with the base malts to get the alcohol you want, but most of the flavour is going to come from the hops.'

Sometimes, however, da Silva will be in unfamiliar territory, working with a style he doesn't know well, as in the case of their Berlin weissbier: 'Those cases are a little bit different,' he says. 'I'll do a ton of research before doing one of those beers, before we even so much as open a bag of grain. From blogs to professional brewing forums to home-brewing sites to see what people are doing. I have a few friends who are professional brewers, and we can bounce ideas off each other. If they have done some particular beer, they may have an insight.'

But whether it's a new style, or one he knows well, 'I spend a lot of time making a recipe before we ever brew it.'

Even when he's brewed a beer successfully, he continues to modify his recipes, for both his special releases and for the portfolio of four beers that he produces on a regular basis for the brewery. 'With our IPA, from the day we opened we have modified the grain bill. We took out a bunch of caramel malt – to make it simpler, to be honest – but also to make the hops come out a little more.' The process is gradual for da Silva, one of first recognizing a shortcoming and then correcting it – but not so much that he turns customers off. 'If they like it,' he says, 'you don't want to change it completely.'

▶ Adding hops while brewing Thirsty Lady American Pale Ale at Heidenpeters Brewery in Berlin. Scribbled hop measurements in a beer recipe.

Mild ales

In its day, mild was the most popular beer in the England, even more popular than bitter. But after the Second World War, it gained a stigma: an association with cloth caps and racing whippets that made it seem old-fashioned, and it began a very long decline. This is a shame because it was a full-bodied, lightly hopped drink and at 3 per cent ABV a great 'session' beer (in other words, one where you can spend a few hours in the pub putting them back without being reduced to a state of leglessness). Originally, 'mild' referred to its age – it was a young (or mild) beer. Later on it referred to the fact that it was mildly hopped in comparison to bitter.

Mawkin Mild ABV: 2.9%

MILL GREEN BREWERY, EDWARDSTONE, SUDBURY, SUFFOLK, ENGLAND

Neil Walker of CAMRA was quoted in the *Daily Telegraph* singing the praises of this beer, made by a craft outfit that calls itself 'Probably the Greenest Brewery in the world'. For a taste of this rare treat, though, you'll need to make your way to Suffolk – it is available in only two pubs.

Ring Your Mother 1832 XXXX Mild ABV: 9%

BUXTON BREWERY, BUXTON, NOTTINGHAMSHIRE, ENGLAND

Forget the bit about legless. This cooperation between Buxton and Dutch breweries Oedipus and Rooie Dop has an ABV approximately three times what milds had 50 or 60 years ago. A resurrection of a nineteenth-century mild, it reminds us how much British beers were modifie and weakened in the early years of the twentieth century. Featuring hints of brown sugar, bread, nuts and figs, one reviewer called it 'a stew of classic English taste sensations on steroids'.

Scottish ales and wee heavy

In technical terms, what makes a Scottish ale a Scottish ale is soft water and a lengthy boil during brewing – long enough that the wort begins to caramelize. The result is a malty beer with a high alcohol content.

BELGIUM

McChouffe ABV: 8%
BRASSERIE D'ACHOUFFE, ACHOUFFE, BELGIUM

'Victorious in battle, Belgium the brave!' Not what we think when we think of Belgium, but why not? The Belgians are masters of beer and apparently they love their Scottish ales. This celebrated take on a wee heavy from one of Belgium's best breweries features notes of raisins, treacle and dates – but the beer finishes nearly bone-dry.

CANADA

Holy Smoke ABV: 6.25% IBU: 25
CHURCH-KEY BREWING COMPANY, CAMPBELLFORD, ONTARIO

Perhaps because the base flavour of any wee heavy is so rich and malty, there is something about this particular style that encourages brewers to think of ways of augmenting it. In the case of Holy Smoke, that means brewing with plenty of peat-smoked malt, giving this rich, dark brew a flavour akin to a crofter's vest.

Innis & Gunn Rum Aged ABV: 6.8%
INNIS & GUNN, EDINBURGH, SCOTLAND

Baked apple? Yes, along with rum and prunes or plum. Innis & Gunn are famous for beers that are 'supposed to taste like one thing, but then we shove it in an oak barrel so it tastes like some other thing'. The idea is that the beer picks up flavours of the barrel's previous occupant. In this case it works, with the hints of rum marrying well with this beer's dark molasses flavour.

Jacobite ABV: 8% IBU: 23
TRAQUAIR HOUSE, INNERLEITHEN, PEEBLESHIRE, SCOTLAND

Traquair House claims the distinction of being the oldest house in Scotland – going back some 900 years. Based on a suitably antique recipe, this is a big, chewy beer with a lot of complexity – we're talking malt, but also coriander and molasses. You would think one such beer would be enough, but Traquair House also produces another wee heavy: Traquair House Ale.

Backwoods Bastard ABV: 10.2% IBU: 50
FOUNDERS BREWING COMPANY, GRAND RAPIDS, MICHIGAN

Fans of this wee heavy make a lot of its bourbon-influenced aroma and flavour. Hardly surprising, given that it is aged in barrels that formerly held Kentucky's greatest export. Available only in November, this brew features aromas of vanilla, and brown sugar, and flavours of whisky and dark fruit.

Barley wines

Numerous tales abound as to the origins of barley wine, a close relative of old ales and winter warmers, but what does seem certain is that a Burton-based brewer named William Bass brought a commercial version to market under the name No. 1 Barley Wine in 1903. Oddly, though, it took the craft brewing movement to bring the style into greater prominence – 70 years later and 8000 miles away. Fritz Maytag, famed saviour of San Francisco's Anchor Brewing, brought out a version called Old Foghorn in 1975. Despite a minor renaissance in the UK in recent years, the American version continues to dominate. Some British drinkers still associate barley wine with its less-than-flattering nickname of 'stingo', its sale in tiny bottles called nips, and its classification as a sitting-down beer (because that meant less distance to fall).

At heart, a barley wine is a straightforward English-style pale ale brewed to a high ABV, often with heavy hopping, and a long ageing period. American brewers have developed a number of variations on the theme, including ageing in barrels and adding a hint of *Brettanomyces*. Annual versions are often released in late autumn as the weather turns chilly. Owing to the high alcohol content, barley wine can – and probably should – be aged after release.

Bodger's Barley Wine ABV: 8.5%
CHILTERN BREWERY, AYLESBURY, BUCKINGHAMSHIRE

Selected by *The Independent* as a top autumn beer in 2011, Bodger's is brewed in the style of a very strong IPA with pale Maris Otter malt and loads of classic British hops Fuggles and Goldings for aroma. Bottle-conditioned, it is golden-chestnut in colour, and malty, citrusy and spicy when it's young. Ageing it for up to a decade helps develops notes of marmalade and Madeira.

Fuller's Vintage Ale 2015 ABV: 8.5%
FULLER SMITH & TURNER, CHISWICK, LONDON, ENGLAND

This is one for ageing. Earlier vintages have won high ratings, and the brewer boasts this one uses all-British ingredients in honour of the 50th anniversary of Maris Otter, the classic British ale malt. It starts off well with aromas of fruitcake and marzipan.

No. 9 Barley Wine ABV: 8.5%
CONISTON BREWING COMPANY, CONISTON, CUMBRIA, ENGLAND

Cask-conditioned to develop a smooth, warming character, this annual brew pours copper with good clarity. It has low carbonation, middling to full body, and flavours of cognac-soaked raisins, dried or candied fruits, toffee, apple, honey and a hint of marzipan. Herbal notes in the aroma are driven by Goldings hops and a warming bitterness emerges that helps balance the sweetness.

UNITED STATES

Behemoth Blonde Barley wine
ABV: 10.5%

3 FLOYDS BREWING COMPANY, MUNSTER, INDIANA

This highly praised, non barrel-aged barley wine wins approval for its integration of hops with a complexity of flavours, including toasted almonds, caramel, cherry and vanilla and a roasty, almost charred finish. The hops flavours vary with vintage and ageing from muted and earthy to prominent and citrusy. It pours ruby or amber with distinct cloudiness.

Bigfoot ABV: 9.9%

SIERRA NEVADA BREWING COMPANY, CHICO, CALIFORNIA

A pioneer – when the brewer introduced it in 1983, the government insisted it be labelled 'barley wine-style ale' to avoid confusion, a convention that's stuck ever since. Still a leader, it has perfect balance of malt sweetness and piny hops, enhanced by dark fruit, butter and caramel notes. Ageing mellows the hops' bitterness.

Bourbon County Brand Barley wine Ale ABV: 12.1%
GOOSE ISLAND BEER COMPANY, CHICAGO, ILLINOIS

Bourbon barrel-ageing mellows this barley wine without dominating it. It pours dark brown with tons of dark fruit (figs, raisins, plums, cherries) and all kinds of other notes: vanilla, brown sugar, caramel, coffee and oak. Rich and sweet, with a thick mouthfeel and low carbonation, this is a beer improved by ageing to smooth its alcohol heat.

Winter warmers

Occasionally known as strong ales, winter warmers are essentially a grab-bag category of dark beers with fairly low malt and relatively high alcohol content, but with considerably lower carbonation levels than pale ales, for example. The brewers sometimes add spices such as cinnamon and cloves. Some, but not all, of these strong ales are true seasonals, available only in wintertime. These aren't beers for tossing back – they are meant to be savoured in a snifter, preferably by a warm open fire on a dark wintry night.

NORWAY

God Jul ABV: 8.5%

NØGNE Ø, GRIMSTAD

From the land that gave us Edvard Grieg and A-ha comes this strong beer available only in winter. God Jul (meaning 'Good Yule' in English) pours dark brown with a fairly impressive beige head and aromas of roasted malt, cocoa and even coffee. Flavour-wise, we are talking espresso, more chocolate, and raw maltiness with a hint of something like charcoal, smoke or even charred malt underneath. The alcohol is not obvious in the tasting.

St. Peter's Winter Ale   ABV: 6.3%
ST. PETER'S BREWERY, BUNGAY, SUFFOLK, ENGLAND

Another personal favourite, sadly this is available
only in the chilly months. It's sometimes also known
as an old ale. Smooth, mildly carbonated, St. Peter's
Winter Ale has a subdued hop character, as you
might expect in a beer like this. There are aromas of
raisins and dark fruit notes combining with flavours
of sweet malt, toffee caramel and hints of spiciness.

UNITED KINGDOM

Odell Isolation Ale   ABV: 6%
ODELL BREWING COMPANY, FORT COLLINS, COLORADO

Odell boasts a very high reputation for good beer,
and this one is great. It pours a beautiful amber-red
colour. There are aromas of earthy hops, cookies and
suggestions of chocolate. 'Cake-like' is one of the
descriptions that people toss around for the flavour,
along with malt, biscuit and caramel. Isolation Ale
finishes slightly bitter, thanks to the hops.

UNITED STATES

4

Wheat Beers

Brewing with wheat

▶ A weissbier must be at least 50 per cent malted wheat – and a lot of them are more.

Malted barley is really the go-to grain where beer-making is concerned, for a number of reasons. But brewers can (and do) use plenty of other grains to brew beer – oats, rye, rice, sorghum in parts of Africa and, most of all, wheat.

Wheat has been used in brewing since the earliest days – the first beers brewed in Sumeria were a mixture of barley and wheat – or, to be correct, the ancestors of those grains. Malted wheat in a beer contributes to a pleasant, viscous mouthfeel and gives the brew a colour and a citrusy taste that can only be described as 'sunny'.

There is, however, a drawback to brewing with wheat. Over the millennia, humans have modified wheat to make it good for making bread by getting rid of its husk and boosting its proteins and glutamates. When mixed with water, malted wheat becomes soft and gummy and can plug a brewing vat completely. But there is a way to brew with wheat – mix it with malted barley, and that is what wheat beers do.

Today there are three separate wheat beer styles: German, Belgian and American, although, as with everything in the world of craft beer, these styles aren't confined to their nations of origin.

Germany

German wheat beers have traditionally been
associated with Bavaria, where they are known as
Weissbierre literally 'white beers' – an allusion to
their pale colour. Once endangered by the tidal wave
of lager that rolled over the world beginning in the
nineteenth century, they began to make a comeback
in the 1960s, and today they account for about 10 per
cent of German beer sales.

A weissbier must be at least 50 per cent malted wheat
– and a lot of them are more. This has a profound
effect on their aroma, flavour and mouthfeel, but
being made with such a high proportion of malted
wheat is not their only unusual quality. Weissbiers
are also characterized by the *weizen* yeasts used in
their production, which produce their trademark
clove flavour as well as hints of banana, bubblegum
and even smoke. In fact, in Germany, outside of
Bavaria, these beers are known as *Hefeweizen,* literally
'yeast wheat', a nod to the important role that the
traditional *weizen* yeast plays in their production.
This is almost a more logical name for them – in the
Bavarian tradition, these beers can also be made with
much darker malts, which produces beers that are
paradoxically known as *Dunkelweizen* (dark wheat).
What matters is not the colour, but the amount of
wheat and the correct type of yeast. And although
they are the most famous, weissbiers are not the only
German beers made with wheat.

Reinheitsgebot

Some people call it the earliest consumer-protection law in the world. On 23 April 1516, Wilhelm IV, duke of Bavaria, issued a decree concerning the purity of beer produced in his realm. Worried about competition between bakers and brewers for wheat, and about crafty beer-makers adulterating brews with unpleasant, or dangerous, additives; he declared that henceforth 'no other items be used for beer than barley, hops and water.' Brewers who failed to meet those standards couldn't call their product beer.

Later called the Reinheitsgebot, the law was modified over time (ironically, a scant decade later malted wheat was included as a permissible ingredient, as was yeast in the late seventeenth century – once people became aware of its existence). The law was later extended to cover all of Germany, although the national version was weakened in the 1980s, when the European Court decreed that foreign brewers were allowed to sell non-conforming beer in Germany – and still call it beer.

For a long time, the law kept competing beers out of Germany, and prevented German brewers from using adjuncts such as corn and rice to stretch their grain bill. But in steering them away from using fruit, spices and other unusual ingredients in brewing, it probably steered them away from innovation.

▲ A maypole paying homage to the traditional purity laws of Reinheitsgebot at Munich's Viktualienmarkt, a daily farmers' market held in the town square.

Belgium

While German wheat beers were threatened in Germany in the 1950s and 1960s, their Belgian equivalents, *wit biers* or *bières blanches* ('white beers') – a venerable style that could trace its lineage back to the Middle Ages – were actually wiped out.

Due to the lager invasion, they were gone by the 1950s, when they were revived by Pierre Celis, who began brewing a beer he called Oud Hoegaards – and ultimately Hoegaarden – after the town where it was made. Flavoured with spices, including coriander and Curaçao orange peel, probably the most unusual aspect of these beers is that the wheat used in them isn't malted.

This contributes to their flavour and mouthfeel, but doesn't give the yeast much to work with. The result is a beer with a refreshing tartness and a cloudy appearance – thanks to leftover proteins and residual yeast. The style caught on in North America, too – particularly in Quebec, Canada, where pioneering craft brewery Unibroue created a version of these Belgian beers they call Blanche de Chambly. So profound is its impact on that province's beer scene that to this day no Quebec craft brewery worth its salt would dream of not brewing a Belgian-style wheat beer.

American

A typical 'American' wheat beer (we'll dig into that a little bit more later) commonly features about 30 per cent malted wheat and, unlike its German or Belgian counterparts, is brewed using standard ale or even lager yeasts.

A classic example of this is MillerCoors' adamantly uncrafty Blue Moon Belgian White, created to capture that part of the domestic market that had been won over by Hoegaarden.

▼ The Allagash Brewery, Maine, USA, produces a variety of traditional Belgian-style white beers.

Many American brewers toss around terms like *Hefeweizen* without actually producing authentic versions of that beer. Having said this, however, there are craft brewers in the United States who turn out good examples of Belgian and German wheat beers.

St. Bernardus Wit Bier ABV: 5.5%

BROUWERIJ ST. BERNARDUS NV, WATOU

This beer was developed for the St. Bernardus Brewery by Pierre Celis, the man who revived the *wit bier* tradition back in the 1960s. It pretty much epitomizes the Belgian *wit bier* style: bottle-conditioned, with aromas of coriander and citrus, a great mouthfeel and cloudy orange colour, thanks to the unmalted wheat.

BELGIUM

Troublette ABV: 5%

BRASSERIE CARACOLE, FALMIGNOUL

The legendary Alström Brothers of the Beer Advocate website sum this beer up succinctly: 'what a Belgian *wit* is supposed to be; dry and yeasty, fruity and spicy with flavours all over the place [sic]'. Coriander and orange peel, combined with a crispness and a slick mouthfeel. There are hops in there, but strictly to balance the malt.

Blanche de Chambly ABV: 5%

UNIBROUE, CHAMBLY, QUEBEC

Another one of the 'beer zeroes', Blanche de Chambly was the first Belgian-style live yeast beer in North America, and set a standard that Quebec brewers have strived to match. Unibroue's 2004 sale to Sleeman broke craft-beer fans' hearts (especially when Sleeman was itself bought by Japanese giant Sapporo), but this is still a fine example of its type, featuring a peppery spiciness and a dry finish.

CANADA

Barrels

Traditionally, beer was fermented in barrels and transported in them as well (the way IPA sloshed about in the barrel on the long trip to India was supposed to be a key part of its fermentation process). Thick enough and tight-seamed enough to withstand the pressure of the carbon dioxide inside, oak barrels were heavy and relatively costly to produce. From the 1950s onwards, traditional wooden barrels have slowly faded away to be replaced by aluminium or stainless-steel kegs that are cheaper to make and easier to clean.

Today, however, wooden barrels are making a comeback and it is not unusual to see a stout or a pale ale advertised as 'barrel-aged'. That word '-aged' is key. These beers are not actually fermented or stored in barrels: 'They are not pressure-proof,' explains Mark Wilson, brew master for Abita Brewing Company in Louisiana, 'the carbon dioxide leaks right out'.

Abita is a leader in barrel-aged beers. 'We use bourbon barrels because they add to and enhance the flavours of our beers,' he says. According to United States' law, all bourbon must be aged for at least two years in oak barrels – these barrels must be new and they cannot be refilled with bourbon. During the bourbon's long maturation, the alcohol actually soaks deep into the barrels' oak staves.

'The beers we've barrel-aged have been mainly stronger beers – an imperial stout, a Baltic porter. We've done a rye pale ale. That may not sound that strong but the viscosity of the rye really stands up to the bourbon. We did a maple pecan beer and the flavours blended in with the flavours from the barrel really well.' Abita's barrel-aged beers are brewed like any other, aged for several weeks and then shifted over to the bourbon barrels for up to two months, before being pumped into bright tanks and then bottled or kegged.

Abita uses each barrel just once. 'You can use them again,' says Wilson, 'but at that point you'll no longer be getting the flavours of bourbon, you'll be getting them [flavours] just from the wood, and they'll take a lot longer to extract.'

▶ A cooper at the Schmid barrel factory assembles a wooden barrel destined to hold beer at the upcoming Oktoberfest, Munich's biggest beer festival.

Side Launch Wheat ABV: 5%

SIDE LAUNCH BREWING COMPANY, COLLINGWOOD, ONTARIO

French-Canadian brewers have embraced Belgian styles, so perhaps it's only fitting that their English-Canadian counterparts go with a German style instead. This tasty take on a weiss hits all the right notes – banana, cloves, even lemons, paired with an amber-gold cloudy appearance.

GERMANY

Ayinger Bräu Weisse ABV: 5.1%

PRIVATBRAUEREI FRANZ INSELKAMMER KG / BRAUEREI AYING, AYING, BAVARIA

Yes, it has some banana, it has some banana today! Talk to the experts and that's what they say you'll find in Ayinger Bräu Weisse – some will tell you it's in the aroma; others, in the taste; still others say it's somewhere in the finish – combined with the weiss' trademark clove taste. Brewed in the town of Aying, this embodiment of the weiss tradition has won plenty of accolades from Wine Enthusiast to *Imbibe* magazine.

Der Weisse Bock ABV: 8.5%

MAHRS BRÄU, BAMBERG, BAVARIA

This is a weiss take on a *bock* beer. It boasts the deep, rich, tawny colour we expect from a bock, but it also features a lot of the cloudy particle matter you'd expect in an unfiltered weiss. A high-alcohol beer, this weiss features a strong malty taste with a fair bit of upfront sweetness, along with cloves and what some drinkers describe as a 'banana bread' flavour.

Weihenstephaner Weissbier

ABV: 5.4%

BAYERISCHE STAATSBRAUEREI, FREISING, BAVARIA

This is the oldest working brewery in the world – dating back to 1040. Weihenstephaner Weissbier is characterized by the usual qualities we associate with *hefeweizen*: cloudy orange colour, hints of cloves and other spices, and a slight banana flavour. After a thousand years in the business, you could probably brew whatever you want and rely on hype to sell it, but this is the real thing.

Weisse Hacker-Pschorr ABV: 5.5%

HACKER-PSCHORR, MUNICH, BAVARIA

Hacker-Pschorr should know what they are doing – they have been at it since 1417. This is another great example of the weiss style. Packaged in a smart swing-top bottle, it pours a nice orange colour with a good head that lasts. It has all the characteristic weiss qualities, but the note that sets it apart from other weissbiers is the mouthfeel – maybe it's the carbonation or maybe it's the wheat, but there is a nice little oomph when you take a good sip.

UNITED STATES

Allagash White Beer ABV: 5%
ALLAGASH BREWING COMPANY, PORTLAND, MAINE

Maine's Allagash Brewing Company was specifically set up to brew Belgian-style beers. This is their version of a traditional Belgian white beer, and features aromas of coriander and pepper and flavours of barley, wheat and spices, notably coriander.

Bell's Oberon ABV: 5.8%
BELL'S BREWERY, GALESBURG, MICHIGAN

Plenty of American brewers put together respectable German and Belgian wheat beers today, but this is an undeniably American take on a wheat beer (albeit without sliding into the sweet, cloying territory that the most popular exemplars have staked out). Brewed with Bell's house ale yeast, this summer seasonal mixes spicy hops with fruity flavours.

Gumballhead ABV: 5.6%
3 FLOYDS BREWING COMPANY, MUNSTER, INDIANA

This hoppy concoction from the estimable 3 Floyds combines wheat with tons of Amarillo hops used in the dry hopping. Widely acknowledged as a truly great beer, it's wheat beer all right, but it really owes more to the American pale ale tradition than to anything you'd find in Bavaria or Belgium.

Ramstein Winter Wheat ABV: 9.5%
HIGH POINT BREWING COMPANY, BUTLER, NEW JERSEY

High Point Brewing Company was created
specifically to create German-style lagers and
ales. Among them is this Winter Wheat, a highly
rated weizenbock. Their website is a little coy on
the subject, but it seems to be made with proper
weizen yeasts. This potent brew, characterized as
having deep, full flavours of caramel and chocolate
combined with the warming effects of alcohol (not
surprising, given its ABV), is available only from
November to January.

▲ Hops ready
for brewing at
Odell Brewing
Company, Fort
Collins, Colorado.

5

Porters
& Stouts

Porters

Porters are dark beers with flavours that are often characterized as bready, biscuity and toasty, with hints of caramel, sometimes nuttiness and even toffee.

As a distinct style, they date back to the eighteenth century. There are numerous legends surrounding their origins, all of varying degrees of improbability; it seems likely that the first porters evolved out of English brown beers. They were brewed using very dark malts that had been dried over open fires. The fires roasted them very dark and possibly imparted a smoky flavour to some of them. Brewers sometimes added liquorice, burnt syrup and other ingredients, too, to get the right colour and flavour.

One unusual quality of those early porters was that they were aged for months in large wooden vats that might have held *lactobacillus* bacteria and wild yeasts such as *Brettanomyces*, which would have given them a sour flavour. Porters became popular at the dawn of the Industrial Revolution in Britain and the brewers of these beers were truly large-scale industrial enterprises.

There are stories of London porter brewers throwing dinner parties for 100 guests inside one of their tuns. On 17 October 1814, a porter vat at Meux and Company in London burst, releasing more than

600,000 litres of ageing beer. The eruption set off a domino effect, rupturing other tuns, tearing out a wall in the brewery and flooding the nearby streets with more than 1,470,000 litres of beer. Two houses were destroyed and eight people drowned in the malty inundation. Eager crowds slurped up the beer as it ran down the gutters.

It's hard to know what those old-time porters really tasted like. In the late-eighteenth and early-nineteenth centuries, brewers began using much paler malts to make beer. The reason for this was pragmatic – these indirectly kilned malts had more usable starch to turn into sugar than those early ones that had been dried over open fires, resulting in more beer for the same amount of malt.

Since then, porters have been brewed using these pale malts with the addition of what are called 'black malts', those that have been roasted to make them very dark and give them the right colour and flavour (sometimes they even add roasted barley). This represents a profound break with the past.

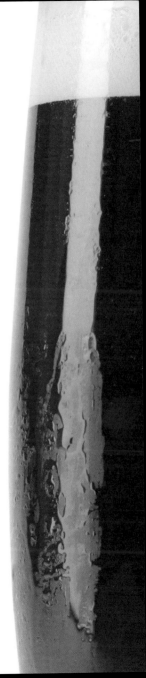

Stouts

Stout evolved from porter. The word 'stout' was often used historically to designate a stronger version of the beer style: originally what is now known as stout was called 'stout porter'. (Porter was so popular that brewers came up with variations on it to capture different markets.)

In time, stout porter came to be known as its own beverage, simply called stout. On its own, stout has evolved in a number of interesting ways – there are oatmeal stouts, so-called milk stouts (brewed with the addition of lactose, a sugar that yeast cannot consume) and imperial stouts, a very strong version of the beer brewed for export to Russia, where a taste for it had developed at the court of Catherine the Great.

These latter stouts spawned imitators in Sweden, Finland, Estonia and elsewhere; local brewers in those countries call these 'Baltic porters', although, as they are in fact made with lager yeasts, they aren't really porters – or stouts – at all.

▲ A vintage advert for the world's best-known stout: Guinness Finest Extra.

When porter began to decline, stout fared a little better in the late-nineteenth century, notably thanks to Guinness (what is commonly called a 'dry stout'), but it too started a long, slow fade. In recent years, however, both porter and stout have been enjoying a revival as craft brewers have rediscovered old porter and stout styles – and even created some new ones, taking this venerable drink in unexpected directions.

AUSTRALIA

4 Pines Stout ABV: 5.1%
4 PINES BREWING COMPANY, MANLY, NEW SOUTH WALES

This stout comes from the brewery that gave us the first beer to be drunk in space. The flavours here are chocolate, coffee and caramel notes from the malt used in the brewing process. These are matched with a balancing bitterness and a full-bodied, smooth finish. Good in the winter (and probably in deep space) with a stew or a chocolate pudding.

Russian Imperial Stout ABV: 9.5%
MORNINGTON PENINSULA BREWERY, MORNINGTON, VICTORIA

Craft brewers have gone crazy for Russian Imperial stouts in recent years, pushing the flavour and alcohol content so far that the line between them and barley wines is blurring a little. This one earns incredible accolades – it's one of the few beers where people seem to discuss not just the flavours so much as the levels of flavour, including liquorice and fruit, building upon one another.

CANADA

St-Ambroise Oatmeal Stout ABV: 5%
MCAUSLAN BREWING, MONTREAL, QUEBEC

McAuslan is one of the pioneers of craft brewing in Canada, and they have been turning out this highly rated oatmeal stout since 1991. Stephen Beaumont, the dean of Canadian beer writers, once rated this the best craft beer in Canada, period. Even today, when breweries and styles have proliferated and there seems to be a stout around every corner, this velvety, inky-dark beer can still hold its own.

Black Perle ABV: 3.8%
WEIRD BEARD BREW CO., EALING, LONDON, ENGLAND

The beard reference tells you that you are on hipster turf here, but dismiss these guys at your peril – they are doing very interesting beers. Perle here refers to a German hop that is often used in stouts. This beer, called a milk-and-coffee stout, is interesting because in addition to adding lactose, they add coffee beans to this stout while it ages. You'll not be dozing off with this in your hand.

Famous Taddy Porter
ABV: 5%
SAMUEL SMITH BREWERY, TADCASTER,
NORTH YORKSHIRE, ENGLAND

If Black Perle represents the cutting edge, Famous Taddy represents reclamation. First brewed in 1979, it is possibly one of the earliest revivals of porter in the twentieth century. Famous Taddy is a classic English porter, characterized by chocolate and coffee aromas, a slightly roasted, tangy flavour and creamy, smooth mouthfeel. The late British beer writer and demi-god Michael Jackson (not that one) called it 'one of the world's five best beers'.

UNITED KINGDOM

Samuel Smith

Founded in 1758 and owned by the Smith family since 1848, the Samuel Smith Old Brewery, or just plain Samuel Smith's as it is commonly called, is the oldest brewery in Yorkshire and one of the oldest in the United Kingdom.

'We're proud of our heritage,' says Sam Smith, who works as an area manager at the brewery and is the fifth generation of the family to be involved with the firm. 'Proud of these wonderful old styles of beer that we have been brewing for going on one hundred years.'

To this day, Samuel Smith ferments all of its ales in what are known as Yorkshire squares, literally large square boxes made of slate that are designed to keep yeast in suspension during fermentation. 'These are the originals,' says Smith. 'They have been in the brewery for over 100 years. They give our beers an incredible body.' To get water for brewing, Samuel Smith relies on its own well, sunk into a limestone aquifer in the eighteenth century. 'It is ideal for brewing ales.' The brewery also employs a full-time cooper, whose job is to build and repair the barrels they use for the cask ales they sell in

their 200 or so pubs, and the brewery's team of grey Shire horses are, says Smith, 'out there five days a week, making local deliveries.'

But Samuel Smith is more than an exercise in nostalgia. 'We started brewing organic beers about 15 years ago,' says Smith. 'We were very much pioneers, and all our beers but one are vegan-friendly. We're very proud of that.' They also continue to expand their offerings. The company recently launched a stout made with organic cocoa, 'and it's really taken off. It's been a phenomenal success.'

Perhaps their most influential idea, however, was the decision to start selling into the United States in the late 1970s. 'Craft beer didn't exist at that point,' says Smith. 'American beers were quite boring and bland. Suddenly along came our beers – our famous pales ale, our IPAs, our porters, our nut-brown ales. I don't want to overstate this, but our beers were revolutionary. We opened a lot of people's eyes and inspired a lot of people to open breweries. Those beers of ours are still revered as benchmarks, godfathers, if you will of those styles.'

▶ The Old Samuel Smith Brewery, Tadcaster, England.

Meantime London Porter ABV: 6.5%

MEANTIME BREWING COMPANY, GREENWICH, LONDON, ENGLAND

Founded in 2000, Meantime was bought by brewing monster SAB Miller in 2015, reason enough for purists to dismiss it. I agonized, but decided to include their porter. This beer features four separate malts, one smoked, and is the traditional strength of a true London porter. Toasty, earthy and smoky, this is one you might want to keep and age – that is, if you have the self-control!

Old Engine Oil ABV: 6%

HARVIESTOUN BREWERY, ALVA, CLACKMANNANSHIRE, SCOTLAND

Harviestoun claims this beer is a black ale, but informed opinion treats it as a porter, so it is included here because it has all the markers – the coffee, the toffee, the chocolate – of what might be called the porter experience. Harviestoun works a variation on Old Engine Oil they call Ola Dubh 30 ('*ola dubh* means 'black oil' in Gaelic). For this one, they boost the alcohol content to 10.5 per cent in the brewing and then season it for six months in old whisky barrels.

UNITED STATES

Edmund Fitzgerald Porter ABV: 6%

GREAT LAKES BREWING COMPANY, CLEVELAND, OHIO

Great Lakes is a brewing company with an awesome reputation, and plenty of people will tell you this is their flagship – appropriate for a beer named after the legendary freighter. This fine porter, with its flavours of roast malted grain and chocolate, has garnered plenty of accolades over the years, and is a five-time medal winner at the Great American Beer Awards.

Founders Porter ABV: 6.5%
FOUNDERS BREWING COMPANY, GRAND RAPIDS, MICHIGAN

Grand Rapids is another one of those towns, like Hershey, Pennsylvania, that is known for brewing craft beer. There are more than 40 craft breweries in and around this charming little city, and Founders is one of the best. The company refers to this as a 'robust' porter; it is considerably more hop-forward than its modern English cousins.

Hunahpu's Imperial Stout ABV: 11%
CIGAR CITY BREWING, TAMPA, FLORIDA

You want scarcity? Cigar City only releases this imperial stout on the second Saturday in March and then only at its brewery in Orlando. Named after Hun Hunahpu, a prime figure in Mayan mythology who (among other things) was slain by the Dark Lords and morphed into a cacao tree, this imperial stout is typified by notes of chocolate, espresso, tobacco, cinnamon and even hints of chilli.

Hill Farmstead Everett Porter

ABV: 7.5%

HILL FARMSTEAD BREWERY, GREENSBORO, VERMONT

The Hill Farmstead Brewery is a family affair, run
out of an old family farm. This porter is part of their
extensive 'ancestral' series, a series of beers named
for their grandfather's thirteen brothers and sisters.
Everett is a rich chocolate and creamy toffee porter
made of American malt, toasted British and German
malts and Columbia hops, which are known for their
earthy, herbal character.

KBS Founders Stout   ABV: 11.2%

FOUNDERS BREWING COMPANY, GRAND RAPIDS, MICHIGAN

If you miss that Hunahpu release from Cigar City
Brewing, don't despair – you may have time to head
north to Grand Rapids and catch the once-a-year

release of Founders' KBS (Kentucky Breakfast Stout), a beer that *Paste* magazine called 'the king of imperial stouts'. Aged in Kentucky bourbon barrels and stored in disused mines beneath the streets of Grand Rapids (I'm serious), the barrels' boozy influence is balanced by flavours of chocolate and coffee.

Mayflower Porter   ABV: 5.2%
MAYFLOWER BREWING COMPANY, PLYMOUTH, MASSACHUSETTS

The word on this one is what you see is what you get. They promise porter and you get that – without vanilla or any other weird add-ons. That said, it's intriguing to check out some of the ingredients: five separate malts (including one that has a smoky peat quality), and a hop boasting the appropriate name Pilgrim.

North Coast Old Rasputin   ABV: 9%
NORTH COAST BREWING COMPANY, FORT BRAGG, CALIFORNIA

For some reason, big stouts sometimes seem to walk hand in hand with difficulty of purchase – available for just one hour, usually at the end of a long-rutted mountain trail, with a limit one dipperful per customer, and so on. So here's one that is excellent and widely available year-round. This gold medal winner at the 2014 World Beer Championships pours black with a tan head, offers up notes of roasted malt aromas and tastes of burnt malt and dark chocolate.

6

Lagers

The beer that conquered the world

▶ Lager doesn't have the most sophisticated reputation, but this golden and hoppy brew with a great white, fluffy head has a lot to offer.

Lager, for the older among us, it is probably what we cut our beer-drinking teeth on in university or at a party in a friend's run-down flat. We didn't expect much from it and it certainly seemed to oblige. Pale-coloured, watery and above all inoffensive, when we spoke of beer this was what we meant. And geographically it was everywhere – all across Europe, dominant in pretty much every corner of North America, the default beer of Asia and Latin America. You could call it the beer that conquered the world. Incredibly, even today, with all we hear about super-hoppy pale ales, imperial stouts and fantastic saisons, lager is still number one – nine of every ten glasses of beer drunk on this planet are lager.

The rise of lager is an incredible story. It begins with Duke Albrecht V of Bavaria in 1553. Concerned that beers brewed during the summer months tended to go bad faster than those made in the cold winter months, he decreed that henceforth, in his happy realm, beer would be brewed only between 29 September and 23 April. (When did governments give up worrying about worthwhile problems like this and start concentrating on trivialities like the economy and foreign affairs?) Of course, people still drank beer in the summer – to keep beers during the warm summer months they would need to be stored in caves often filled with ice cut during the winter. But here's where it gets really interesting: almost all

the beers in Europe at this time were brewed with varying strains of a yeast known as *Saccromyces cerevisiae* (good old ale yeast to us). This is what made – and continues to make – our pale ales, stouts and so on. This yeast ferments at warmer temperatures, and when it's fermenting it creates a sort of crust on the top of the beer. These yeasts are called top-fermenting as a result.

Accounts differ, but from somewhere outside of Europe (theories vary as to where), a new yeast showed up, one that had a particular quality – it thrived at low temperatures. The details of the yeast romance are impossible to describe adequately, but somehow, *S. cerevisiae* and the mystery yeast met, loved each other very, very much, and a new hybrid yeast – *Saccharomyces pastorianus* – was born. This was a yeast that could thrive at low temperatures, temperatures at which *S. cerevisiae* was in virtual suspended animation.

At some point, this new yeast met ideal conditions in the Bavarian caves. And a new beer was born – this beer took longer to ferment, but was far clearer than any ale. It was also a yeast that didn't produce the wacky esters that *S. cerevisiae* did. These beers were more about the flavours of the ingredients than any chemical side effects from fermentation.

Lager grew more and more popular in Bavaria and it started to spread, helped along by the new railways that were spreading across Europe. The great wave of German immigration that started in the middle of the

nineteenth century (and accelerated after the failure of the revolutions of 1848) saw German lager-makers reaching the shores of the United States.

Lagers could be anything from golden verging on black. What made a lager a lager was the yeast. The beer that we have in mind when we think of lager emerged in the late-nineteenth century in a town called Plzen or Pilsen in what is now the Czech Republic. They had the yeast, they had a particular hops called Saaz and they knew about what the British had developed in terms of creating light-coloured malts. They combined these to make the pilsner, a golden, hoppy beer with a great white, fluffy head.

▲ The ornate gates of the Pilsner Urquell Brewery in Plzen, Czech Republic, the famed birthplace of pilsner lager.

When brewers in North America tried to replicate this beverage using the available barley, they found that there was a lot of residual protein that gave the beer a cloudy look. But this leftover protein could be used to ferment the sugars in so-called adjuncts – rice and especially corn, which made it cheaper to brew beer – creating an inoffensive beer that anyone could enjoy.

In 1873, a clever German academic named Carl van Linde, working for one of the German breweries, developed the first artificial refrigeration system. You didn't need caves or ice houses; now, you could make lager anywhere in the world – from Tierra del Fuego to India's coral strand. The lager that conquered the earth was born.

We might be right to dislike this brew; we might be right to dislike what it did to the world of beer. But it isn't lager's fault – a young and impressionable beverage, you could say it fell in with bad company. The Germans never gave up on lager and if you take the time to learn about it, you soon understand there is a lot more to it than the pallid stuff with 'beer-like' qualities that beer snobs sneer at. Lager is almost a universe of beer styles unto itself.

AUSTRALIA Dogbolter ABV: 5.2%
MATILDA BAY BREWING COMPANY, HOBART, TASMANIA

As mentioned, a lager can be any colour – it's the yeast and nothing else that determines whether a beer is lager or not. In this case, the chocolate malt and chocolate wheat used in the brewing make it dark. Matilda Bay was Australia's first-ever craft brewery and this was one of their first beers.

Knappstein Reserve Lager
ABV: 5.6%
KNAPPSTEIN ENTERPRISE BREWERY AND WINERY, CLARE, SOUTH AUSTRALIA

This is the first, and so far only, beer offering from Knappstein. Maybe it reflects the firm's wine-making heritage but this Bavarian-style lager has hints of aromas and flavours you might expect in a wine – lychee, grapes and other fruit. Perhaps this is due to the Nelson Sauvon hops, so named because they impart a fresh, crushed-gooseberry flavour similar to that found in Sauvignon Blanc.

Samichlaus Classic Bier ABV: 14%   AUSTRIA
BRAUEREI SCHLOSS EGGENBERG, VORCHDORF, GMUNDEN

Reputed to be one of the strongest beers in the world, this is also one of the rarest, being brewed only one day a year, on St Nicholas Day, 6 December. The beer is aged for ten months before bottling. This deep ruby-red *doppelbock* features aromas of plum, raisin and dried fruit, followed by a sweet and fruity, creamy mouthful with an alcohol burn. Suitable for ageing, after a few years it develops a creamy, smooth finish.

Urban-Keller Steinbier ABV: 5.6%
BRAUHAUS GUSSWERK, SALZBURG

Vienna lagers first appeared in 1841. The Vienna malt, darker than that used in pilsner, produced an amber lager with a dominant flavour described as bready or toasty. They aren't seen much in Austria today, however. This example is also unusual in being a steinbier, literally 'stone beer.' During brewing, hot stones are dropped into the wort to bring it to the boil, caramelizing some wort in the process.

CANADA Captivator Doppelbock
ABV: 8%
TREE BREWING COMPANY, KELOWNA, BRITISH COLUMBIA

A doppelbock is literally twice the bock, a high-alcohol version of this traditional beer. In keeping with bock tradition, Captivator is available only in springtime. It pours a deep amber colour, and features a unique note of banana in its aroma. There are notes of caramel and toffee in the beer's flavour. Definitely worth a trip to the British Columbia interior.

Cerna Hora ABV: 5%
L'AMÈRE À BOIRE, MONTREAL, QUEBEC

When the wave of lager washed over North America, Quebec, in particular its French-speaking citizens, resisted and kept drinking ales. So it's surprising to see this. Sadly, to experience it you'll have to go to Montréal – no hardship – to drink it at L'Amère à

Boire, the brew pub that makes this dream. Munich malt, Saaz hops and the right yeast make this a true Czech(-style) pilsner.

Koutská 12° Dvanáctka ABV: 5%
PIVOVAR KOUT NA ŠUMAVĚ, KOUT NA ŠUMAVĚ

The Czechs rate their beers according to the Plato scale, which, among other things, tells you how strong a beer is, with the scale running from 0°, in theory, right up to 18°. A 12° beer is at the premium end of the scale. This highly regarded pilsner, made with Saaz hops, comes from a small brewery in western Bohemia not far from the German border.

Lobkowicz Knight ABV: 4.8%
PIVOVARY LOBKOWICZ, VYSOKÝ CHLUMEC

Another 12° beer, Lobkowicz Knight is characterized by a biting hop taste, combined with flavours of grainy malts and a nice finish. Pretty much everything one would want in a pilsner, coming from a brewery founded in 1466. While the brewery was nationalized by the Communists after the Second World War, in 1992 American-born and raised William Lobkowicz succeeded in getting back ownership of the family brewery and now runs it.

CZECH REPUBLIC

X Beer 33 ABV: 12.6%
U MEDVÍDKŮ, PRAGUE

It sounds more like a spacecraft than a beer, but X
Beer 33 is proof that the Czechs aren't only about pale
pilsners. This behemoth of a beer pours a deep ruby-
red, almost purple, with a thin head. A sweet beer,
it boasts aromas of flowers and fruit, and there are
hints of plum in the flavour, all set off with an almost
oily mouthfeel.

ETHIOPIA Bedele Beer ABV: 4.25%
BEDELE BREWERY, BEDELE

Bedele is a fairly small place, about 483 km from
Addis Ababa. Bedele Beer may be made in east
Africa, but its heart is firmly in Bohemia. This is
a sweet, malty pilsner balanced by piquant and
floral hops that would go very well with spicy
wat and *injera*.

GERMANY Aecht Schlenkerla Rauchbier
Märzen ABV: 5.1% (VARIES BY YEAR)
BRAUEREI HELLER-TRUM, SCHLENKERLA, BAVARIA

Rauch in German means 'smoke', and that hits the
nail on the head. *Rauchbiers* are made with green
malt that is smoked over a fire of beechwood logs.
Forget the classic beer-tasting talk about subtle hints
of this or notes of that – this is all about the smoke. By
analogy, this beer is probably closer to smoked meat
or jerky than any other flavour you can think of.

Andechser Spezial Hell ABV: 5.8%
KLOSTERBRAUEREI ANDECHS, ANDECHS, BAVARIA

In German beers, the term lager generally refers to a
beer that has been aged for a while. A young version
of the popular pale golden beer is referred to as a
Helles (meaning pale). Helles come from Bavaria;
and this well-balanced example is from the town
of Andechs and is made in a brewery attached to a
Benedictine monastery.

Augustinerbräu Lagerbier Hell
ABV: 5.2%
AUGUSTINERBRÄU, MUNICH, BAVARIA

The Augustiner-Bräu Wagner has been making beer
since the fourteenth century. This brewery is one of
what are sometimes referred to as Munich's 'big six',
and one of just two of those that are still independent.
This fine example of a Munich Helles has hints of grass
and hay in the aroma. Grass and hay are present in
the tasting too, along with a bready flavour. The hops
are nicely bitter, but not overwhelming.

Ayinger Celebrator Doppelbock
ABV: 6.7%
FRANZ INSELKAMMER KG / BRAUEREI AYING, BAVARIA

The '-ator' ending (see also Captivator in Canada
above) is a long-time naming custom with bocks.
Ayinger has been producing this since 1878, when
it was originally known as Fascinator. We're talking
toffee, caramel, dark-roasted malt flavours – all with
that really clean taste we associate with lagers.

Ayinger Leibhard's Kellerbier
ABV: 4.9%
PRIVATBRAUEREI FRANZ INSELKAMMER KG /
BRAUEREI AYING, BAVARIA

Kellerbieren (cellar beers) are unfiltered lagers that
are stored for a very long time at low temperatures.
Because they are unfiltered they are (relatively
speaking) quite cloudy for lagers, and they are often
a deep amber in colour, sometimes with a reddish
tinge thanks to the caramelized malt used in their
creation. This example from the Ayinger brewery
mixes yeasty, bready, malty flavours with a herbal
hoppy bitterness and features the great kellerbier
mouthfeel: smooth with low carbonation.

EKU 28 ABV: 11%
KULMBACHER BRAUEREI AG, KULMBACH, BAVARIA

Another doppelbock, EKU's website refers to this as
a stout – it is, but only in the traditional sense that
any strong beer is called stout. Lagered for a full nine
months at temperatures touching on freezing, EKU
28 (the 28 is a reference to the beer's degrees Plato) is
characterized by flavours of caramel, fresh bread and,
of course, alcohol.

Hacker-Pschorr Oktoberfest Märzen ABV: 5.8%
HOFBRÄU MAIBOCK, HACKER-PSCHORR, MUNICH, BAVARIA

Historically, *Märzen* was a strong beer brewed in
March (hence the name), and then stored in caves
over the summer. It was also traditionally the beer

of Oktoberfest and sometimes these beers are in fact called Oktoberfests rather than Märzens. The style is characterized as malty to begin with, but dry on the finish, with hop bitterness but no real hop flavour.

Hofbräu Maibock   ABV: 7.2%
HOFBRÄUHAUS, MUNICH, BAVARIA

As the name suggests, *Maibocks* were bock beers traditionally brewed in May. They had the higher alcohol content of a bock, but were lighter in colour than real winter-brewed bocks. For this reason they are sometimes also known as Helles bock. Hofbräu's Maibock offers aromas of honey and sweet bread and follows up in taste with more of the same, plus some spicy hops and a sweet finish.

Mahr's Hell   ABV: 4.9%
MAHRS-BRÄU, BAMBERG, BAVARIA

Another fine example of a Munich-style Helles, featuring aromas of what seem to be pears and honey, and the toasty bready flavours associated with this style. The mouthfeel is summed up with a single word – creamy – and the finish is bone-dry. A few years back, the magazine *Men's Journal* called Mahrs-Bräu, 'the finest brewery in the world' and this Helles is one example of why they thought so.

Cask versus keg

For the casual beer drinker, it is sometimes hard to understand when people talk about beer in a cask versus beer in a keg. We are often told that cask ales are generally supposed to be good, but also that the bulk of beer comes in kegs.

What is the difference? And why is there a difference? 'The main difference,' says Andrew Connell, one of the owners of Halifax, Nova Scotia's Bar Stillwell, a destination for serious cask-ale fans in eastern Canada, 'is the service style'. Both kegs and casks are made out of stainless steel, but a keg is designed to 'allow CO_2 or nitrogen to be pumped into the cask, so that the beer can be pushed through beer lines and come out through a tap'.

With a cask, however, no gas is used to remove the beer: 'They come to us sealed,' says Connell, who learned his craft working at the famed White Horse pub in London, which typically offered 15–20 cask beers. 'Twelve hours before serving, we tap a small piece of wood called a spile into the shive bung [a small plastic seal].' Once the seal has been broken, the beer can be pumped out.

The differences between keg and cask beer are more than the delivery system. Keg and cask beers are profoundly different in nature – even the same beer is different depending on whether it's been kegged or casked.

If a brewer is filling kegs, Connell says, 'they would run their beer into a bright tank [the tank where fermented, filtered beer is held prior to packaging]. It would [then] be ... carbonated, and then put into a keg'. With a cask, the brewer could follow the identical brewing process but 'instead of sending it to the bright tank, they would run it into casks with some priming sugar. Any yeast remaining in that beer will ferment that sugar and create its own carbonation inside the cask'.

The result is a beer that is far less carbonated – particularly because the cask is opened hours before it is drunk. 'A lot of people tasting cask for the first time will think they are tasting flat beer – but it's just the traditional low-carbonated style'.

Some of the most interesting things about cask beers are the flavours they develop. 'That extra fermentation that goes on inside the cask can create nice fruity esters that might have been cut short in transferring the beer to the bright tank. In beers that have fruity hop flavour those fruity yeast esters can be really complementary and the way that beer tastes can be really different from the way it tastes on tap [drawn from a pressurized keg].'

'Another cool thing about cask is that you can dry hop cask beers pretty effectively, say actually putting a bag of fresh hops inside to give a really nice

aroma to the beer'. Not all beers work well in casks, though. '[It's] completely appropriate for English milds or bitters. [It's] completely inappropriate for Belgian styles, say saisons or Abbey beers, which are supposed to be highly carbonated.'

The major drawback to casks is oxidation, a side effect of opening them which can cause them to go stale. 'The effects can be seen in a couple of days,' says Connell. 'With kegs, you're just sending CO_2 or nitrogen in there, and they can last a lot longer.'

For true beer obsessives, nothing compares to cask. 'I don't think you'll find anyone out there who loves beer and doesn't love cask. They kind of go hand in hand.'

Mönchshof Schwarzbier ABV: 4.9%

KULMBACHER BRAUEREI AG, KULMBACH, BAVARIA

It's a lager, but it's as black as a glass of Guinness.
These black beers were traditionally brewed using
Munich and dark-roasted malts, and today many are
done with husked roasted malts to avoid some of
the acidic flavours that are a challenge with darkly
roasted malts. This particular *Schwarzbier* has an
interesting note of chocolate in its flavour.

Neumarkter Lammsbräu Organic Pilsner ABV: 4.8%

NEUMARKTER LAMMSBRÄU, NEUMARKT, BAVARIA

Sometimes with organic beers you suspect that
the important thing is that they are organic – and
that any flavour is an afterthought. This beer is an
exception – not only is it organic, but it also garners
loads of praise, including a 99 out of 100 from the
folks who run the Beer Advocate website. This pilsner
features aromas of bread and dried citrus. Sipping
it, you notice Noble hop bitterness, which is nicely
balanced by the malt.

Pfungstädter St. Nikolaus ABV: 6.9%

PFUNGSTÄDTER BRAUEREI, PFUNGSTADT, HESSE

First developed in the town of Einbock, bock beers
are higher in alcohol content than most lagers.
Not particularly hoppy in nature, they range in
colour, generally from golden to amber, although St.

Nikolaus pours a dark brown. A sniff of St. Nikolaus gives you aromas of sweet malt, earthy and herbal hops that carry over into the actual taste of the bock.

Rothaus Pils Tannenzäpfle

ABV: 5.1%

BADISCHE STAATSBRAUEREI ROTHAUS, GRAFENHAUS, BADEN-WÜRTTEMBERG

This pilsner has a bit of a cult status in Germany: a fairly cheap, but also very good beer, brewed in a state-owned brewery – a baffling idea to anyone from the English-speaking world. It pours a clear, bright pale yellow with a nice frothy head and offers up aromas of hops and grass. There's that nice German malt flavour and it finishes with a good hop bite.

Weihenstephaner Original

ABV: 5.1%

BAYERISCHE STAATSBRAUEREI, FREISING, BAVARIA

That the first-ever mention of hops was at the monastery in Weihenstephan in 768 should give you an idea of how deep the brewing traditions runs here. Their Wiehenstephaner Original is widely regarded as the example of a Munich-style Helles. It has aromas of lemon and biscuits fresh from the oven, and a taste that manages to combine those two flavours with a nice yeasty oomph.

JAPAN Koshihikari Echigo Beer ABV: 5%

**UEHARA SHUZOU CO. LTD / ECHIGO BEER PUB,
NIIGATA-KEN NISHIKANBARA-GUN**

Japan's first craft brewery and brew pub, Echigo,
opened its doors in 1994. They produce styles we
associate with the craft-beer boom such as pale
ales and imperial stouts, and they have won a few
international awards over the years. This lager is
brewed with Koshihikari rice, a premium short-
grain variety grown in Nigata prefecture. We're not
talking explosive flavours here – this is a delicate
and balanced version of a uniquely Japanese take on
lager, where rice is not used as a cheap adjunct but as
a deliberately featured ingredient.

NETHER-LANDS Emelisse Rauchbier ABV: 6.2%

**BIERBROUWERIJ EMELISSE, KAMPERLAND,
NOORD-BEVELAND**

This is a subtler Rauchbier than a lot of others. Oh,
it's smoky all right, but the sensation that you're
licking an old ashtray is delightfully absent. If
there is such a thing as smooth smoke, the Emelisse
Rauchbier has it. An opaque dark brown or amber
in colour, with a fruity aroma, this beer gives tastes
of sweet maltiness, bitterness and smoke.

La Trappe Bockbier ABV: 7%

BIERBROUWERIJ DE KONINGSHOEVEN, BERKEL-ENSCHOT

This particular bock comes from the sole (and very
highly regarded) Dutch brewery run by the Trappist
order. This is the only bock brewed by Trappists

anywhere – they generally prefer Belgian ale styles. This particular bock pours a deep reddish brown with an incredible tan head that stays and stays. There are aromas of dark fruits, caramel and a bit of hops and those all follow through in the flavour, joined by toasted malt and even molasses.

Camden Hells Lager ABV: 4.6%
CAMDEN TOWN BREWERY, CAMDEN, LONDON, ENGLAND

Did no one ever think of this before? This one is half Helles, half pilsner, all inspired. What these guys have done is take the pilsner malt used to brew a pilsner, but then hop it with Perle and Hallertauer, the two hops traditionally used to brew Munich Helles. Then they aged it like a lager. An inspired idea.

Curious Brew ABV: 5.6%
CHAPEL DOWN WINERY (BREWED BY HEPWORTH),
TENTERDEN, KENT, ENGLAND

Chapel Down has the distinction of being the largest winery in England and has recently branched out into beer-making as well. This prize-winning pilsner is double-fermented – first with a standard lager yeast and then with a champagne yeast – giving it, in the words of beer writer Peter Brown, 'a delicious grapey fruitiness and tingling sparkle'. Before bottling, it is hopped again and then filtered.

UNITED KINGDOM

UNITED STATES

Brooklyn Lager ABV: 5.2%
BROOKLYN BREWERY, BROOKLYN, NEW YORK

If you want an idea of how far the craft-brewing scene has come in the last quarter-century, then you need look no further than Brooklyn Lager. When it was introduced back in 1989, this dry-hopped amber brew, created using an old lager recipe from the turn of the century, was a revolutionary upstart in the world of pale American corporate lagers. Hoppy and citrusy, it can still hold its own today.

Capital Autumnal Fire ABV: 7.8%
CAPITAL BREWERY, MIDDLETON, WISCONSIN

Capital Brewery was founded 30-plus years ago, specifically to brew German-style beers. It has branched out considerably over the years, but, given that early emphasis, it's not surprising that the brewers at Capital can turn out an excellent doppelbock: Autumnal Fire. Brewed each September, this coppery bock is characterized by sweet, malty aromas and notes of toffee and dark fruit.

Eliot Ness   ABV: 6.1%
GREAT LAKES BREWING COMPANY, CLEVELAND, OHIO

You'll sometimes see American brewers refer to
their Vienna-style lagers as 'pre-Prohibition style',
hailing back to the time when American lagers were
darker and hoppier (and tastier). This well-regarded
example invokes the name of Eliot Ness, the head of
the famous 'Untouchables', who battled Al Capone
in the 1920s and hung out in what is today the
brewery's taproom.

Mama's Little Yellow Pils   ABV: 5.3%
OSKAR BLUES BREWERY, LYONS, COLORADO

No, it's not just here because of the name – although
it is pretty good. You might call this a craft take on
the standard American lager. The big difference – and
it is a profound one – is no use of adjuncts such as
rice or corn syrup. This all-grain version of a pilsner
uses Saaz hops to give it a strong bite on the finish.

Prima Pils Lager   ABV: 5.3%
VICTORY BREWING COMPANY, DOWNINGTOWN,
PENNSYLVANIA

The general consensus on this pilsner is that it is far
hoppier than is typical for the style. Not that there's
anything wrong with that – beer styles should be
played with and tested. The reason probably lies in
the use of whole-flower German and Czech hops.
There are malt flavours in there as well, but in this
beer they play second fiddle.

7

Belgian Beers

Belgium: a nation, not a style

Belgium is a nation, not a style, but there is something about Belgium that, beer-wise, sets it apart, that demands that it be treated on its own. Some of it may be their yeasts – top-fermenting at warmer temperatures, they produce spicy and fruity flavours that often combine in complex ways – and Belgians are always willing to take their chances with whatever is out there in the open air or lurking in the wood of an old barrel. Or maybe it's their daring contrariness. Most brewers worldwide fear *lactobacillus* as a spoiler of beers; the Belgians worked with it to give their beers a sour flavour. Or maybe it's their 'toss it in' attitude. When it comes to what goes into the wort they are astonishingly open. Pale malt? Sure. Wheat? You have it. Candi sugar? Certainly. Dark sugar? Makes great dark beer. Pepper, spices, star anise – and the list goes on and on.

Whatever it is, Belgian beers are an epiphany. The flavours, the effervescence, the aromas. Apart from their *wits*, which we have dealt with elsewhere, their beers resemble nothing else on Earth (and even the *wits* are unique). No Belgian beer has every attribute listed above but they all have some. In the English-speaking world, even after the rise of craft, Belgian beers were not well known until the late 1990s, but once beer drinkers discovered them, they couldn't get enough. And today, brewers all over the world are doing their best to imitate them.

▶ An innovative menu board at a Belgian beer bar in La Roche-en-Ardenne, Luxembourg.

Flanders red ale & Oud Bruin

With their dry finish and tannins (and colour), it's not too hard to see parallels between these red ales and red wine. No hop aroma or flavour, although there is some bitterness. Their strongest elements are maltiness and sourness that play off against each other. *Lactobacillus* and *Brettanomyces* play key roles in the final flavour.

Oud Bruin style has its roots in east Flanders and can be traced back to the 1600s or so. Reddish-brown to brown, it boats aromas of malt and fruity esters. These are echoed in the flavour, along with some caramel. Bruins are made with a base of Pils malt. They gain their dark colour thanks to additions of dark cara malts and a dash of black or roasted malt.

BELGIUM

Duchesse de Bourgogne ABV: 6%
BROUWERIJ VERHAEGHE, VICHTE

These red ales are often called the Burgundy of Belgium, so it is fitting to name one after Mary, Duchess of Burgundy, who ruled the country in the fifteenth century. A blend of eight- and eighteen-month-old oak-aged beers, the end result is a deep red brew that boasts aromas of dark fruits and malty sweetness along with a sourness like vinegar. The flavour combines a tart, cherry-like taste and a lot of oakiness from the barrels, with a fresh, pleasant aftertaste.

▶ Crates of Grand Cru beer at Rodenbach brewery, Steenhuffel, Belgium (see overleaf).

Monk's Café Flemish Sour Ale
ABV: 5.5%

BROUWERIJ VAN STEENBERGE, ERTVELDE

This Oud Bruin pours dark brown, and features pungent and tart aromas, with the dominant taste described as either tart or sour. With a medium body and moderate carbonation, this beer has an interesting provenance. Long known as 'BIOS – Claamse Borugone' and apparently only brewed once a year, Belgian-beer enthusiast Tom Peters, owner of Philadelphia's Monks, convinced the company to produce it for him under his private label.

Rodenbach Grand Cru   ABV: 6%
BROUWERIJ RODENBACH, ROESELARE

Flanders red ales are usually blends of new and older beer. Eugene Rodenbach seems to have learned the technique during a spell as an apprentice in England in the 1870s. The version of this red ale known simply as Rodenbach is largely young beer, while Grand Cru is mostly older beer; after blending it is aged in oak barrels for two or more years, emerging a crisp, dry, refreshingly tart beer.

UNITED STATES

The Dissident   ABV: 10.7%
DESCHUTES BREWERY, BEND, OREGON

Widely regarded as one of the best American takes on the Oud Bruin style, The Dissident is brewed using Montmorency cherries and dark candi sugar, then aged in barrels for 18 months. First brewed in 2008, The Dissident has so far been released every other year.

Lambics

Lambics are truly the moment when Belgian beers pass through the looking glass. In their basic ingredients, lambics resemble a lot of other Belgian beers, in that they contain many unmalted wheat. And like most beers elsewhere, they do contain hops – but old hops (in their case, several years old) that often possess 'cheese-like' aromatics. No matter – their job is to prevent spoilage, not to add flavour.

Where they really differ, however, is in their fermentation: the breweries that create lambics let them ferment naturally in large open vessels called coolships, fermented with whatever strain of *Saccharomyces* falls in, along with who knows what flora found in the brewing equipment and the

▼ The Belgians take lambics so seriously that there's a museum dedicated to them: Bezoekerscentrum 'De Lambiek', Alsemberg. Belgium.

brewery itself. Then *lactobacillus* work away at them, turning sugars into lactic acids and contributing to the beer's sour taste. The final stage in a lambic's fermentation occurs in the oak kegs where it is stored for months or even years, home to the wild yeast *Brettanomyces*. This gives the lambic its trademark flavours of horse blanket and hay barn, but also tropical fruit and peach.

Like many Belgian beers, lambic beers are typically blends. *Gueuze* (or *geuze*) is a mixture of new and old lambics where a secondary bottle fermentation is kicked off by the sugar present in the younger of the two. *Kreik* is made with the addition of fruit, usually cherries, and left to ferment for six months.

BELGIUM Cantillon Grand Cru Bruocsella (1900) ABV: 5%
BRASSERIE CANTILLON, BRUSSELS

Today, Cantillon is the only lambic maker actually located in Brussels itself, not in the outlying area. Grand Cru is somewhat unusual in that it is a true lambic. That means funky aromas and farmhouse flavours combined with a tartness like that of a very sour white wine. And like a wine, this beer is very nearly flat.

Hanssens Oude Kriek ABV: 6%
HANSSENS ARTISANAAL, DWORP

Pours a deep cherry colour with a neat, slightly pinkish head. There are plenty of cherries in the aroma too, along with lactic acid and sourdough. These beers are so connected with their particular brewery and location that each one has a distinct flavour; Hanssens is no exception, its distinct essence gives their beers a sharp edge.

Lindemans Gueuze Cuvée René
ABV: 5.5%
BROUWERIJ LINDEMANS, VLEZENBEEK

Lindemans blends lambic that has aged for at least two years with beer that is at least a year old. Cuvée René features aromas of must and chalk that mingle with green apple and vinegar. An initial tartness on tasting gives way to flavours of fruit – apple and tart red fruit – and dry malt. An excellent gateway gueuze for the first-time imbiber.

Allagash Coolship Resurgam
ABV: 6.3%
ALLAGASH BREWING COMPANY, PORTLAND, MAINE

UNITED STATES

Given the intimate connection with place that is so much a part of lambic brewing, can a beer really be a true Belgian lambic if it isn't brewed in or around Brussels? Resurgam is exposed to wild yeast, aged just like a Belgian lambic, and then blended in a similar fashion – in Portland, Maine. Still, the beer has won its share of awards, including a Bronze at the 2013 Brussels Beer Challenge, so they seem to be doing something right.

Pale ales

These beers are fairly similar to their British counterparts, although as always with the Belgian beers, they have a different yeast character and more varied malt profile. Although they are called Speciales, they are really everyday beers, the session beers of Belgium, especially in the provinces of Antwerp and Brabant.

BELGIUM

De Koninck ABV: 5.2%
BROUWERIJ DE KONINCK, ANTWERP

This cloudy amber beer is truly the beer of its hometown, Antwerp. This is very much a typical Belgian pale ale, almost a little too mainstream for inclusion here, but still worth mentioning – if only as a comparison to the other stronger versions of the types. Fragrant aromas are followed by a great biscuit or toasted malt flavour, smooth and clean on the palate.

Duvel ABV: 8.5%
BROUWERIJ DUVEL MOORTGAT, BREENDONK-DORP

A strong Belgian pale ale (it's not called the Devil for nothing), Duvel pours cloudy and pale, but keeps its head when all about are losing theirs. Smooth and creamy, with a very dry finish, Duvel's aromas include citrus and there is a yeastiness there too. Malty sweetness and yeasty tartness jostle with each other in the taste.

La Chouffe ABV: 8%

BRASSERIE D'ACHOUFFE, ACHOUFFE

Another strong version of a Belgian pale ale, La Chouffe (a play upon their town's name, d'Achouffe – *chouffe* means gnome in the Walloon dialect), is characterized as variously crisp, dry, snappy and effervescent. However, the quality singled out repeatedly in this pale ale is spicy – cloves, maybe; pepper, for sure. There are some fruity flavours like peach in there too.

▼ Brasserie d'Achouffe, Belgium

Farmhouse ales

Farmhouse ales were beers brewed by farmers (often in what were termed farmhouse breweries) during the winter months for consumption in the summer. Generally, there were two kinds of farmhouse ales. *Bières de garde* (beers for keeping) were commonly produced in France, in the departments of Du Nord and Pas de Calais (although the Belgian province of Hainaut also turned them out). The Belgians went with saisons, meant to be drunk by the temporary 'seasonal' workers in the summer. Both beers are characterized by a certain cellar taste and are very dry. The BJPC guidelines define the dominant difference as being 'that the bière de garde is rounder, richer, malt-focused and lacks the spicy, bitter character of a saison.'

BELGIUM Saison Dupont ABV: 6.5%
BRASSERIE DUPONT, TOURPES

Take a sniff and you'll get aromas of cellar with notes of pear and something herbal. This is a crisp and dry beer, with mild tartness and flavours of dry grain mixed in with a funky cellar taste that makes you long to find the Flanders farm where they keep this one.

Saison de Pipaix ABV: 6%

BRASSERIE À VAPEUR, PIPAIX-LEUZE

Black pepper, ginger, sweet orange peel, Curaçao –
those are just a few of the spices the brewery loads
into this great saison. Those spices come out in the
aromas and in the taste, where they combine with the
saison's trademark earthiness. And you have to love a
beer made by a brewery that proudly identifies itself
as still being steam-powered.

3 Monts Flanders Golden Ale

FRANCE

ABV: 8.5%

**BRASSERIE DE SAINT-SYLVESTRE, SAINT-SYLVESTRE-
CAPPEL**

France has produced but one (albeit very good) beer
style, the bière de garde. This highly carbonated
beer pours a beautiful golden colour and produces
a creamy white head. There are aromas of straw,
pepper (and some say herbal tea) in the beer. It has a
light malt character in terms of flavour, with herbal
and lemon notes and a long dry finish.

Ommegang Hennepin ABV: 7.7%

UNITED STATES

BREWERY OMMEGANG, COOPERSTOWN, NEW YORK

This saison, brewed in the town that is home to the
Baseball Hall of Fame, knocks it out of the park.
Named for the Catholic priest who was the first
European to see Niagara Falls, the beer features a
peppery aroma and a whiff of Belgian yeast, and the
taste, ah! the taste – light and refreshing, with fruity
flavours and a dry malt thing happening.

Trappist

Trappist beers are among the most influential and popular of those brewed in Belgium. To merit the name (and carry the distinct hexagonal Authentic Trappist Product symbol), a beer must have been brewed within the walls of one of Belgium's six Trappist monasteries, either by monks or under their guidance (however general), and the proceeds must be used either to support the order or support social services. Although monks have been brewing beers in Europe for centuries, Trappist beers can only trace their origins back to the 1930s.

Although there is no specific Trappist style (in much the same way there is no specific Belgian style), the beers brewed by the country's Trappists do share certain qualities: they are top-fermented, unpasteurized and brewed without chemical additives, with extra sugar added to the wort to boost the alcohol content and, in bottling, to kick off secondary fermentation. The popularity of these beers has inspired many imitators, who often call their products 'Abbey' beers.

▶ The austere interior of Scourmont Abbey, home to Chimay beers, Ardennes, Belgium.

Many Trappist monasteries also brew beer exclusively for their own consumption. These are generally lower in alcohol than the beers they offer commercially.

Chimay Première (Red) ABV: 7%
BIÈRES DE CHIMAY, BAILEUX, CHIMAY

Trappist beers are typically brewed in three strengths: *dubbel, tripel* and, since the 1990s, *quadrupel*. These refer specifically to the original gravity of the wort before fermentation and generally to their alcohol content as well. This one is a dubbel. One reviewer spoke of an aroma of 'musty spiciness', another of 'spicy mustiness' – you decide. Strong and with great flavours of dark fruit and some mild hoppiness, this is a great example of a dubbel.

BELGIUM

Chimay Tripel (White) ABV: 8%
BIÈRES DE CHIMAY, BAILEUX, CHIMAY

The aromas of this beer are banana and floral, with a hint of almond and something almost medicinal. That slightly medicinal detail carries through to the tasting, where it combines with a hint of bitter almond. Mostly what you notice is the bitterness, and below it all that trademark Belgian-yeast earthiness. This beer is dry in the finish.

St. Bernardus Abt 12 ABV: 10%
BROUWERIJ ST BERNARDUS, WATOU

One of the points that should be made about Abbey beers and other 'unofficial' Trappist knock-offs is that they can be quite good – as good as the originals. St. Bernardus Abt 12 is a case in point. A beautiful, rich mahogany, this well-carbonated beer gives off aromas of malt, cloves and ripe fruit. In the tasting, the malt is there along with the fruit and alcohol, giving way to a slightly bitter finish.

Trappistes Rochefort 10 ABV: 11.3%
ABBAYE NOTRE-DAME DE SAINT-REMY, ROCHEFORT

The 10 in this case refers to the type of beer (these guys make a 6 and an 8 as well), not the alcohol content, which – incredibly – is even higher. This Belgian quadrupel boasts aromas of plum spiciness and brown sugar, a malty, almost molasses-like flavour with an unmistakable warming alcohol effect. Some will tell you this is one of the world's great beers – others find it syrupy and cloying.

Trappist Westvleteren 8 (VIII)
ABV: 8%
BROUWERIJ DE SINT-SIXTUSABDIJ VAN WESTVLETEREN, WESTVLETEREN

The best dubbel in the world? Some people certainly think so. Trappist Westvleteren 8 (VIII) pours a deep chocolate-brown with a rich head that dissipates quickly. There is plenty of fruit and spice to entice the nose and the taste is a sweet malt flavour with some caramel, combined with a creamy mouth feel. If it isn't the pinnacle, it is certainly up there.

8

Discover

Novelties & mysteries

This category comprises a miscellany of beers: some, like Kölsch and steam beer, have a highly respectable history but an unusual brewing technique, while others are as new as tomorrow – if they survive that long. This is all too true of what might be called the 'stunt beers', but who knows, some may have a longer-term impact on the craft industry.

The mash-ups

Kölsch combines top fermentation (normally used for ale) with cold conditioning at a slightly higher temperature than the usual for lager. The yeast is specialized, selected over centuries to accommodate the hybrid brewing technique. Traditionally, both hops and malt are restrained, with the latter sometimes consisting entirely of Czech pilsner malt. The resulting beer is gold, crisp, clean and slightly to moderately bitter, with enough fruity, spicy notes characteristic of other top-fermented brews to give it complexity. Reissdorf Kölsch from Germany's Brauerei Heinrich Reissdorf is a highly rated example. Among American versions, which tend to be a little more adventurous, Samuel Adams East-West Kölsch gets high praise, with a heavier body and more hop character. Note that while kölsch is a distinct style, many brewers lager their lighter ales.

California common, or steam beer, is the mirror-image of Kölsch: a unique American beer using bottom-fermenting yeast that can work at higher-than-normal temperatures. It's the result of brewers' ingenuity when faced with the need to brew beer in San Francisco for the California gold rush in the nineteenth century. Without the European caves in which cold-temperature lagering took place, brewers eventually developed lager yeasts that could survive at warmer temperatures (it may have helped that the Bay area climate is notoriously chilly by California standards). Appropriately, this unique beer style pretty well kicked off modern American craft brewing: in 1965, Fritz Maytag bought into the struggling Anchor Brewing, which was still making steam beer, and the rest is history: Anchor Steam remains one of the top-rated examples of its type. It's described as hazy copper in colour, with earthy, sweetish aromas and a flavour that leads with hoppy bitterness and lemon and ends with highly toasted malt and a citrus finish.

For better or worse, future permutations along the lines of Kölsch and steam beer will undoubtedly be facilitated by the industrial development of new yeast strains and even new enzymes. And new yeasts aren't just coming from the labs. Nor are they all – strictly speaking – new. Beers have been brewed recently using yeasts from the Rogue brew master's own beard, not to mention more ancient sources. Examples include Bone Dusters Paleo Ale, which uses yeast from a whale fossil, and a wheat beer from Fossil Fuels brewed with yeast extracted from amber.

Animal, vegetable or mineral

Many emerging trends and styles depend on adding a variety of stuff to the beer, whether unusual fermentables, botanics or – yes – animal parts. One beer even used a pinch of crushed meteorite. A few of these experiments are taking their place as accepted styles, such as 'Rye PA,' a pale ale in which rye takes the place of some of the barley, and adds spicy notes. It's an updated, hop-forward take on traditional rye-based beers from places like Bavaria, where that grain is more widely grown. RPA from Cameron's Brewing Company, near Toronto, is a well-regarded example.

Many breweries offer a pumpkin-spiced ale as a seasonal fall brew. When brewed as a proper style and not a gimmick, these can be delicious, with a substantial mouthfeel, mellow, sweetish flavour and balance of warm spice. Punkin Ale from Dogfish Head Brewery in Delaware, United States, is widely considered one of the best. Unfortunately, too many – usually brewed with extracts and/or flavourings – are as unpleasant as the ubiquitous scented candles and lattes of the same name.

▶ Belvoir Brewery in Leicestershire, England, adds whey from Stilton cheese to produce their Blue Brew.

Tea may be up next as a serious beer ingredient. While coffee is widely used in porters and other dark beers, interest in speciality teas is leading to craft brewing experiments that range the beer spectrum from the light – green-tea pale ale – to the heavy – chai-flavoured milk stout. With that range and the positive reviews they're getting – a Japanese green-tea pale ale from California's Stone Brewing

"THE KING OF BRITISH ALES"

THE BLUE BREW

Company is rated outstanding – tea may well end up being woven into several popular styles.

The list of other fermentables that brewers are playing with, many of which have a pre-existing history in making alcoholic drinks, is endless. The starches include sweet potato, exotic rices, buckwheat, spelt and chestnuts (the only nut high in starch instead of fat). In Leicestershire, Belvoir Brewery adds whey from Stilton cheese-making to the mash to produce their Blue Brew, which is generally described as tasting actually pretty good.

Among fruits, you can start with grapefruit, dates, mangos, lychees, cranberries, rhubarb, elderberry and pineapple, in addition to the more common additions like raspberries and cherries, and go on and on. Even oily seeds and nuts are getting used, despite the challenges they can present to head formation. Unusual botanicals like Sichuan peppercorns, rose petals, marigolds, bog myrtle, spruce, lemongrass, yarrow, hibiscus and hemp are also finding their way into craft brewing.

Then there are those animal parts that, perhaps surprisingly, ended up in the vat on purpose. Again, some, like whole chickens and oysters, aren't new. But additions like prairie oysters (a regional term for bull testicles), smoked goat brains, a whole pig and whale testicles smoked over a sheep-dung fire certainly appear to be. The last of these, by the way, comes from Iceland, where, one assumes, it's matched with rotten shark, a beloved local snack.

The possibilities are endless, but of course the risk is that brewers' ambitions will outrun their judgement. For example, how about a beer and a nice coconut curry – not served separately at your table, but mixed in the mash? Many food-based beers seem to be flavour-of-the-month phenomena, with efforts to cash in on sometimes fleeting fads like maple-bacon. But if you're interested, there are curry, banana bread, lemon meringue pie and pizza beers, as well as Peanut Butter & Banana Ale and something called Voodoo Doughnut Chocolate.

High-stakes beers

Finally – and after the smoked whale testicles, we could probably all use one of these – there are the high-ABV beers. These beers push the natural limits of how much alcohol yeast can pump out before the booze literally kills it. Techniques include a mix of yeasts and freezing to concentrate the alcohol. At the moment, the reigning high-stakes beer appears to be Snake Venom from Scotland's Brewmeister, which – at an ABV of 67.5 per cent – outranks many distilled spirits. Since it was only in around 2000 that beers surpassed 20 per cent ABV, this kind of progress means that in the none-too-distant future, beers will be 100 per cent alcohol and we can all go home.

Food & beer

When it comes to matching food and drink, there are times when only beer can fit the bill. In all their dry, crisp glory, lager and pale ale really sing with complex, spicy foods. Lesser tipples don't stand a chance. And that same crispness stands up well to the smokiness of charcuterie. Not to mention the starring role that darker ales and lagers play alongside humble homey fare that befits beer's history as a drink of the people. Nor should we leave out the pairing of beer and snacks, which – let's be honest – is probably the most frequent match-up of beer and food. As for what exactly works with what, there are no specific laws. Beers are so splendidly individual that they give you huge scope to experiment. Consider the following as guidance only.

First, should you try to pair the beer at all? Many craft beers have a lot of flavours going on just by themselves. Enjoying them with anything but the simplest food may cause a gustatory clash.

Next, decide whether you want to go for contrasting (bitter against rich, sweet against sour) or complementary (more of everything!) flavours. The stronger the flavours in the beer or the food, the more the pairing might benefit from contrast. I once tried smoked beer with smoked cheese: it was like drinking from an ashtray, then licking it clean.

Another frequent suggestion is colour matching – lighter-coloured beers with lighter-coloured foods and vice versa. Not a bad starting point, but ultimately too limiting. As your matching chops develop, you're likely to find great pairings that fall way outside this box. And it certainly doesn't work with beer and cheese pairing, which is a world unto itself – one I'll visit briefly later.

Matching also depends on how the food is cooked. Roasting and grilling caramelize sugars and bring out earthy notes. Long, slow cooking creates mellow flavours and a softer mouthfeel that might stand up well to a more sharply carbonated beer. Grain-based dishes like couscous, risotto and polenta are driven by their individual textures and other ingredients, which themselves complement or contrast the grain's flavour. You can play around here with beers that also have a lot of notes, or keep it simple and uncluttered.

Finally, the thorny issue of beer with sweets. To some, beer with dessert feels unnatural, stretching to prove a point. Dark chocolate with porter or stout gets trotted out suspiciously often. But try some pairings yourself and see what you think. The whole point is to have a little fun. The following are a few thoughts on specific beer styles and what they might work with.

LIGHT-COLOURED LAGERS

A chilled blonde lager goes down a treat with don-don noodles, biryani or Mexican-style pulled pork, especially on a hot day. If the food is screamingly hot, however, don't go too upscale (or too strong) with the beer – you'll be downing it too fast to savour. For slower sipping, try grazing a platter of Hungarian farmer's sausage, paper-thin smoky Westphalian ham and other charcuterie.

BOCK

If you ever visit the hill country around Austin, Texas, you have to try the local German-influenced beef barbecue. Bock with smoky, slow-cooked brisket is a perfect team.

IPA

IPA's bitterness counteracts fatty foods, keeping your taste buds clear for the next bite. Try it with fish and chips (although not if the beer is too hop-forward), seared duck breast or a juicy burger. Avoid anything too delicate – it'll be overwhelmed.

MID-RANGE ALES AND LAGERS

Highly versatile beers that, if not too extreme in style, can pair with anything from barbecued wings to stuffed squash to beef Wellington.

SAISONS, LAMBICS AND FARMHOUSE ALES

Food with milder flavours will allow the floral delicacy of a lambic, saison or farmhouse ale to shine. Try a dish of roasted fennel, chicken and lemon over a creamy risotto. Or go complementary with roast lamb crusted in coriander, fennel, garlic and orange zest.

FRUIT BEERS

These should taste of the fruit they're made from, but with little or none of the sweetness. The acidity, not the hops, balances the food's richness. A fruit beer would work well in place of a rosé, for example, alongside a simply roasted chicken with a sourdough stuffing, dried fruit and pecans, or a ponzu-glazed pork belly, red rice and bok choy.

BEER WITH NOTES OF SPRUCE AND/OR JUNIPER BERRY

Tangy beers for special meals. A perfect match for braised caribou, or wild boar sausage, or a barley risotto with roasted root vegetable and forest mushrooms.

SMOKED BEER
What's needed is something silky and unctuous that isn't going to fight the smoke. Maybe a creamy roasted corn and potato chowder, or an upscale Welsh rarebit.

STRONG ALES, PORTERS AND STOUTS
These are winter beers, perfect to pair with cold-weather fare: oxtail stew, braised short ribs of beef, maybe even lamb shanks slow-cooked with the same beer, Middle Eastern spices, apricots and prunes.

And let's not forget beer and cheese. According to the experts, they make a more compatible couple than wine and cheese. Here are some quick suggestions, mostly reflecting the approach of contrasting (rather than complementing) flavours, but again, try your own experiments.

LIGHTLYHOPPED BLONDE ALE with notes of spice and orange
Buffalo mozzarella

DRY, CRISP PALE LAGER
Smoked cheddar

AMBER ALE, MID-RANGE LAGER
Medium to mature cheddar

HOP-FORWARD PALE ALE especially with apricot notes
Ten-year-old cheddar

SMOKED ALE
Raw-milk gouda

SAISON OR BIÈRE DE GARDE
Creamy blue

BARLEY WINE OR STOUT
Stilton

Festivals

There are now dozens of beer festivals and beer weeks around the world. This list focuses on some of the longest-running and/or largest.

Oktoberfest, the world's biggest beer festival, attracts millions of visitors to Munich every fall and has spawned many imitators. But nothing is quite like the original.

The Campaign for Real Ale organizes the **Great British Beer Festival** in London every August, featuring close to 400 breweries, with a focus on casked and bottled real ales.

The Knighthood of the Brewers' Mashstaff and the Belgian Brewers put on the annual **Belgian Beer Weekend** in Brussels every September. Close to 50 Belgian breweries, including monastic ones, take part.

Pilsner Fest takes place in Plzen (Pilsen), Czech Republic, in early October to celebrate the day 200 years ago that the first batch of Pilsner Urquell was brewed.

Denver, Colorado, hosts the **Great American Beer Festival**, the showcase for American brewers with more than 3,500 beers on offer, each year in early autumn.

Montréal's **Mondial de la Bière**, in late May, is Canada's largest beer festival and enjoys an international reputation. It has spun off festivals of the same name in France and, most recently, Brazil.

Qingdao International Beer Festival, in the Chinese city that gave us Tsingtao, is Asia's biggest beer festival. Given the size of the potential Chinese market, it's no surprise that brewers from around the world flock to the festival every August. No surprise, either, that large-scale producers dominate.

Great beer destinations known for their bars and breweries:

UNITED STATES & CANADA

Austin, Texas
Boston, Massachusetts
Chicago, Illinois
Cleveland, Ohio
Denver, Colorado
Minneapolis/St Paul, Minnesota
Montreal, Quebec
Philadelphia, Pennsylvania
Portland, Maine
Portland, Oregon
Providence, Rhode Island
San Diego, California

UNITED KINGDOM

Edinburgh, Scotland
London, England

EUROPE

Bamberg, Germany
Bruges, Belgium
Munich, Germany
Prague, Czech Republic

Glossary

ABV (Alcohol by volume) The share of alcohol in a beer as a percentage of its volume. Most beers fall within a range of 4–6%, but some are higher or lower.

Adjunct Unmalted grains, starches or sugars that have been added to a brewing beer. The goal might be to reduce costs by using a cheaper source of sugars for fermentation, or (more often the case in craft brewing) to produce a beer of a particular style or character. Common cost-reducing adjuncts include corn, rice and sorghum. Other adjuncts, like wheat, fruit and pumpkin, are essential to certain styles of craft beer. *See also* malt.

Beer engine A system for raising beer from a cask stored in a cellar to keep it cool, traditionally featuring a handle that is manually pumped. Beer from a keg may use a similar-looking device, but is not pumped manually.

Cask-conditioned Conditioned in a cask. For traditionalists, real ale must be cask-conditioned, neither pasteurized nor artificially carbonated, and served directly from the cask using a beer engine.

Conditioning Secondary fermentation in the cask or bottle that takes place after beer is removed from the primary fermenter. Sugar is often added to kick off secondary fermentation by residual yeasts, but traditional krausening might be used instead, especially in wheat beers and German lagers.

Degrees Lovibond A numbering system that ranks malts in order of colour from light to dark. The weighted average of the degrees Lovibond of the malts in a mash predicts the colour of the final beer. *See also* SRM (Standard Reference Method), EBC (European Brewing Convention) for other methods of ranking colour.

Degrees Plato A measurement system used by brewers, especially in the United Kingdom, for density.

Dry hopping Adding hops to cooled wort after the boil in the primary or secondary fermenter, or even directly to a keg. Dry hopping enhances the flavours and aromas produced by hops, but does not add significant bitterness as the hops are not boiled. *See also* hop character, wet hopping.

EBC (European Brewing Convention) A European scale for classifying the colour of a finished beer. *See also* degrees Lovibond, SRM (Standard Reference Method).

Enzymes Proteins that act as catalysts to speed the transformation of one substance into another. Each enzyme carries out a unique function with a unique substrate: in brewing, the enzymes convert the substrate starch into sugar.

Esters A family of chemical compounds produced by fermentation, especially at the warmer temperatures in which ales are brewed. Flavour notes include banana, apple, anise, pear and nail-polish remover (unfortunately) – the last largely explaining why esters are blamed for some off-flavours.

Fining agent A substance added to beer at the end of the boil or after fermentation to make it clearer. If the fining agent is from an animal source, such as isinglass, the beer is not suitable for vegetarians. Some feel fining may reduce flavour complexity as it clears the beer of particulate matter. *See also* haze.

Flavouring agents Additions to beer that impart specific flavours. European brewers have used agents such as coriander and orange peel for centuries. Craft brewers are delving into the past and ranging further afield with additions including bog myrtle, green tea, spruce tips, lemongrass and jalapeños. Using adjuncts such as maple syrup, honey and fruit also brings distinctive flavours (as well as added sugars) to a brew.

Haze Cloudiness arising from the presence of certain compounds in finished beer, especially proteins and phenols. Haze is widely regarded as undesirable and removed by filtration or fining, but it is a characteristic of many European wheat beers.

Hop character The primary flavour of hops is bitterness, created during the boil as acids in the hops are chemically altered. Specific varieties may also display citrus (especially grapefruit), other fruit (including pineapple and apricot), piny, cedar, and/or floral flavours and aromas. Many beers are defined by the flavours and aromas, as well as the bittering qualities, of the hops used in their production. Perhaps the strongest association is West Coast pale ale and citrusy hops. *See also* dry hopping, wet hopping.

Hop-forward Any beer that is strongly marked by its hop character, especially aroma and/or flavour is considered hop-forward. Hop-forwardness tends generally to be characteristic of lighter-coloured ales, with darker varieties taking more of their flavour from their malts and grains, or their yeast. *See also* hops, dry hopping, wet hopping.

Krausen As a noun, krausen is the layer of bubbly, scummy-looking foam that rises as beer ferments and gives off carbon dioxide, then falls as primary fermentation ends. As a verb, it means adding freshly fermented wort instead of sugar to beer that is ready for conditioning.

Lacing The lacy pattern left on the inside of the glass as the beer is drunk, indicating the quality of the head.

Malt A grain that has been allowed to start sprouting, then heated to stop the process. The purpose is to maximize the enzymes that will convert starch in the grain to sugars. Barley is the most commonly used malt because its structure and chemistry result in highly efficient brewing. Heating malted barley to different temperatures produces speciality malts that are key to flavour, colour and body, especially in mid-range and dark-coloured beers. Malts of other grains, such as wheat, are sometimes added to or substituted for malted barley in particular styles. Grains that have not been malted can work as supplements, but brewing beer without any malt is challenging. *See also* adjuncts, mash, wort.

Mash A mixture of water, crushed malt (usually all or mostly barley) and any adjuncts. *See also* mashing, wort.

Mashing A key stage in brewing, in which the mash is heated in a tun (a large metal vessel) to specific temperatures for specific periods of time to maximize the conversion of starches to sugar.

Mouthfeel An elusive but important element in how beer is perceived. It includes such factors as the beer's temperature, density, viscosity and carbonation. Adjuncts like wheat and oatmeal are valued in creating a distinctive mouthfeel because of the proteins they provide.

Off-flavours Flavours that impair the quality of beer. Some off-flavours, like diacetyl and dimethyl sulphide, are produced naturally in brewing and are even desirable in some beers; others are the outcome of poor sanitation, grain storage and/or brewing practices. *See also* oxidation, esters, phenols.

Oxidation A reaction between wort and oxygen that results in a number of off-flavours, including wet cardboard and sherry.

Phenols A family of chemical compounds. Most phenols that find their way into beer are considered off-flavours – including those of sweaty horse-blanket and sticking plaster – but a few, such as the one that gives Hefeweizen its note of cloves, are desirable.

Specific gravity (SG) The density of a liquid relative to that of pure water, which, at 4°C (39°F), has a specific gravity of 1.

SRM (Standard Reference Method) A North American scale for classifying the colour of a finished beer. *See also* degrees Lovibond, EBC (European Brewing Convention).

Wet hopping The use of fresh, rather than dried, hops in brewing. Although challenging for the brewer because hops are highly perishable, wet hopping is thought to add a clearer, more distinct hop characteristic to a beer.

Wort The sweet solution left by straining the liquid after mashing. Its sweetness comes from conversion of starches to sugars during heating, facilitated by enzymes in the malt. The wort is then boiled for an hour or more, normally with hops, before being cooled. Yeast is added to the cooled wort to start fermentation.

Index

This edition first published in the UK and
Australia/NZ by Hardie Grant Books in 2016

Hardie Grant Books (UK)
52–54 Southwark Street
London SE1 1UN
hardiegrant.co.uk

Hardie Grant Books (Australia)
Ground Floor, Building 1
658 Church Street
Melbourne, VIC 3121
hardiegrant.com.au

Conceived and produced by
Elwin Street Productions Ltd
14 Clerkenwell Green, London, EC1R 0DP
www.elwinstreet.com

British Library Cataloguing-in-Publication
Data. A catalogue record for this book is
available from the British Library.

Cover illustration: East End Ltd
Interior design: Fogdog.co.uk

ISBN: 978-1-78488-063-7

Printed in China

10 9 8 7 6 5 4 3 2 1

MIX
Paper from
responsible sources

FSC
www.fsc.org   **FSC® C016973**

PICTURES: Alamy Stock Photo: Arterra
Picture Library, 115, 123, Aurora Photos, 64,
Cephas Picture Library, 113, David Kleyn,
125, Ed Rooney, 106, Foodfolio, 87, Heini
Kettunen, 16–17, Ian Dagnall, 77, M-Dash,
24–25, Marc Tielemans, 29, Mark Hayes, 76,
Marvin McAbee, 11–12, MSP Travel Images,
81, Peter Forsberg, 91, Randy Duchaine, 44,
René van den Berg, 119, Richard Griffin, 28,
The Picture Pantry, 89, Ton Koene, 58–59,
Westend61 GmbH, 62. AleSmith Brewing,
San Diego, CA, USA, 43. Allagash Brewing
Company, Portland, ME, USA, 117. Ayinger
Privatbrauerei, Aying, Germany, 69. Ayinger
Privatbrauerei, Germany, 98. Bieres et
fromages trappistes de Chimay, Baileux
(Chimay), Belgium, 124. Belvoir Brewery,
Leicestershire, UK, 131. Brouwerij Van
Steenberge, Ertvelde, Belgium, 114. Buxton
Brewery, Nottinghamshire, UK, 49. Camden
Town Brewery, London, UK, 105. Cameron's
Brewing, Ontario, Canada, 41. Tree Brewing,
Kelowna, BC, Canada, 94. Coniston Brewing
Company, Cumbria, UK, 53. Coopers Brewery,
Adelaide, Australia, 30. Founders Brewing
Company, Grand Rapids, MI, USA, 83. Fuller
Smith & Turner, London, UK, 33. Getty Images:
Adam Berry / Stringer, 19, 47 (top &bottom),
Adam Smigielsk, 75, Adermark Media, 36–37,
Altrendo images, 39, Bloomberg, 8, 13, 72–73,
126–127, Craig F. Walker, 71, Dana Hoff, 23,
Dennis K. Johnson, 111, Dirk Olaf Wexel, 31,
Dorling Kindersley, 14, Ed Norton, 108–109,
Helene Canada, 48, Johannes Simon / Stringer,
67, 139, John Greim, 6, Kaz Ehara, 7, Koji
Hanabuchi, 55, Maurice Rougemont, 2–3,
Monty Rakusen, 100–101, Nicholas Kamm,
15, Richard Derk, 85, Tetra Images, 9, 27,
Tony Briscoe © Dorling Kindersley, 61. Great
Lakes Brewing, Cleveland, OH, USA, 107.
Hill Farmstead Brewery, Greensboro, VT,
USA, 84. Klosterbrauerei Andechs, Germany,
97. Knappstein Enterprise Brewery and
Winery, Australia, 92. Mahrs- Bräu, Bamberg,
Germany, 99. Meantime Brewing, Blackwell,
London, UK, 82. Mill Street Brewing Company,
Toronto, Canada, 32. Neumarketer Lamsbrau,
Bavaria, 103. Nøgne Ø det Kompromissløse
Bryggeri AS, Grimstad, Norway, 56. Russian
River Brewing, Santa Rosa, CA, USA, 34.
Samuel Smith Brewery, Tadcaster, Yorkshire,
UK, 42, 79. Sierra Nevada Brewing Co., Chico,
CA, USA, 54. St. Peter's Brewery, Bungay,
UK, 57. Shutterstock: © Christian Draghici,
135, © Cosma, 137. Stone Brewing Company,
Escondido, CA, USA, 35. Traquair House,
Innerleithen, Scotland, UK, 51.